The Missing Piece

....

Juliane Kohl

Contents

----

prologue

"Are you Annalise Manson?" The police officer at my door asks me.

"What's it to you?" I respond wearily, crossing my arms in attempt to come across as more confident, when, in reality, I'm trying not to cower in fear.

"Answer the question, kid." He orders sternly.

I inhale. "Yeah, I am."

He pushes past me, letting himself in and sits down on the ripped up, leather couch.

"Where are your parents?" He inquires. I immediately stiffen.

My dad ran two days ago, leaving me to fend for myself. He couldn't go without beating me one last time though. Whenever I blink, the image of him standing over me, a smirk on his face, after pushing me down the stairs appears in my mind. The memory plays on repeat like a broken record.

"My dad's at work." I lie.

"At 8am?" He counters suspiciously.

I nod. "Why do you need him?"

He exhales, and it's obvious he's contemplating something.

"Your father is in jail." The police officer tells me. "He has been for two days. Early this morning, he confessed to leaving you here and now it's our job to take you to a safe place. A place where you'll be taken care of."

"I can take care of myself. I don't need to go to a foster home where they give me sympathetic smiles and pray before each meal." I argue.

"You won't be going to a foster home." He informs me. I furrow my eyebrows, and he continues. "You have seven brothers, Annalise. Your temporary guardian will be the oldest: Archie, until your father gets out of jail."

And with that, he explains my family history to me. How my father took me away from my mother and brothers when I was only two. How my birth mother died a few years after. And how all of my life has been a lie. Every single moment of it.

My heart aches at the thought of them knowing I've been out here all this time, and they've never reached out. They could have sent me a letter. Messaged me. Called me. Anything. Anything to know that they cared. But maybe they don't.

"When will I go?" I ask.

"Once you've packed your stuff, I'll take you to the train station and your brothers will pick you up from there. Hopefully you'll be settled in by the end of the day." He tells me.

Here's the prologue! Please comment any suggestions and vote for my story, it'd mean the world to me!

Word count: 447.

chapter one - long lost sister

I get off of the train, duffel bag flung over my shoulder.

As I walk through the station, I find that it's mostly empty, apart from the people who also got off at my stop.

Maybe my brothers forgot to pick me up. Or maybe they never intended to in the first place. If I was them, I wouldn't make me a priority either. They don't know me. They only know the old, two-years-of-age me. I'm a stranger to them. And they're all strangers to me.

I'm debating wether to just walk away and break into an abandoned house for the night when a black, limo-looking car pulls up next to me. The drivers window rolls down, revealing a brown haired man with dark eyes.

"Are you Annalise?" He asks.

I nod once, slightly weary. At my response, he looks at me up and down, almost as if he's examining me, searching for any flaws.

"I'm Joseph. Your brothers driver." He explains. "Hop in."

My brothers have a driver?

I know they own a family business, so it must be an incredibly successful one if they've made enough money to employ a driver.

I walk to the back and pull open one of the car doors, shutting it again quickly once I'm sitting on one of the leather seats.

I set my bag down next to me and put my seatbelt on with my right hand, because my left still hurts from when dad pushed me down the stairs. No matter how many times I ice it, and no matter how many painkillers I take, the throbbing won't stop. Not to mention the dark bruise won't disappear. I hope it does quickly, though, because if my brothers find out, it could ruin my fresh start and that is the last thing I want.

For the majority of the ride into my new life, I gaze out of the window, looking at the different people, buildings and trees we pass. There isn't much else I can do to occupy myself. I'd go on my phone, but I avoid it because it's been glitching all day. I'm not surprised it's slowly breaking, it's an old model.

We stop in front of two metal gates that, when opened, reveal a majestic house, no, mansion. It's hard for my mouth not to gape at the sight.

Joseph slowly drives around the large fountain, stopping a few meters away from the front door.

"The door should be open, and a maid will lead you to your room." Joseph explains.

I look over at the house, then down at the car floor. I feel out of place in my ripped up jeans and jumper. If I knew that this place was gonna be as fancy as it is, I would've made a bit more of an effort.

"Thanks, Joseph." I finally say, clutching onto the handle of my bag and climbing out of the car.

Once I'm at the front door and Joseph has driven away, I feel lonely. Lost.

Questions with no answers suddenly flood into my mind.

What if they don't like me? What if they're nice to my face but then talk about me to each other when I'm sleeping? What if they take one look at me and decide I'm not wanted in their perfect family?

I suck in a breath.

What if they're just like dad?

I turn around and as I take my fourth step, I bump into a wall.

I swear there was no wall here.

I look up, and my eyes widen. Not a wall. A man. One of my brothers, I think. I silently pray that he's just someone coming to check their gas or something similar.

The guy looks at me the same way Joseph did.

He furrows his eyebrows slightly, and when he talks, his voice is deep and hardly comes out in a whisper.

"Annalise.."

"Nope, wrong person." I quickly dismiss. As I go to walk away, he grips my injured arm, making it throb however I manage to fight the urge to wince.

I hear the faint sound of a car door shutting and footsteps get closer and closer, until I feel a warm arm on my shoulder, which I'm surprised I don't flinch away from.

"Grayson, careful you don't scare our little sister away within the first five minutes of her getting here." Someone says.

The man who I now know to be Grayson rolls his eyes and walks past me, making his way into the house. I turn around and I'm greeted with light blue eyes as well as a happy smile.

"Hi, I'm Harvey." He tells me.

"Hey.." I mumble.

I imagined what meeting my brothers would be like the whole train ride here. I forgot to take in to account the awkwardness that might occur. I don't think Harvey finds it awkward, though, because he's only staring at me intently with his light blue eyes, as though he's trying to figure me out.

I immediately switch to my expressionless face. The one that hides the way I'm truly feeling.

"Right." He says after a few moments. "Let's go inside."

chapter two - night terrors

T he inside of the house is even more beautiful than the outside. When my ripped up shoes hit the marble floor, the sound echos throughout the house.

There are two sets of spiral staircases opposite to each other, and a family portrait of all my brothers hangs in between them. They aren't smiling, though, their faces are straight and serious. I feel something that resembles guilt when I realise I'm not in it. I don't know why I would be, I'm not really part of their family. I'm blood-related, sure, but I haven't seen these people in eleven or so years.

"When was the last time you ate?" Harvey inquires. When I turn my head, he's already looking at me.

Two days ago. "I ate before I came here. My social worker bought me McDonald's." I lie. Dad wouldn't let me eat anything for long periods of time, but I can't tell him that. If my brothers do end up caring about me, I don't doubt for a minute that if they find out about dad, they'll walk around me like I'm a broken doll, they'll give me sympathetic smiles instead of real ones, and they might even make me go to therapy.

The last thing I want is to be a bother.

"Oh, alright. Are you still hungry?" He inquires.

"No. I'm okay." I respond.

"Okay, I'll show you your room then." Harvey says, and then begins walking to one of the staircases. I have to power walk so that I can keep up with his long strides. I didn't realise that my brothers would be so tall. Grayson was, too.

Once we're upstairs, he walks down a few hallways that I'm sure I'll get lost in, and stops suddenly in front of a white door. I almost run into his back but manage to catch myself before I do.

"Here we are." He announces, gripping the doorknob and pushing it open. My eyes widen in awe when my new room is revealed to me.

The walls are a light grey, a shade close to white, and the floor is carpet. In the middle on the far wall is a grand canopy bed, decorated with violet sheets. A long, marble desk runs against half of one of the walls and there are two doors within the room.

It's plain, but I love it.

"You like it?" Harvey asks.

"I love it. Thank you." I quickly respond, a smile on my face. A real smile.

"I'm glad. I'll leave you to unpack." He says. As he's going to walk out, he turns back. "We have a movie room downstairs, if you wanna watch something later."

My smile becomes brighter.

"Yeah, sure." I respond.

He nods and smiles before leaving, kindly shutting the door behind him.

I look over my room again. I don't deserve this. It's too.. nice.

Despite my thoughts, I throw my bag onto the bed and pull out the blanket I brought from home. I lay out at the end of the bed and get the stuffed animal I've had since before I can remember and set it on my pillow.

I throw the bag under the bed—that's tomorrow's problem—and begin exploring. I don't go into any rooms, though, incase it's one of my brothers rooms and they think I'm snooping. That would be a bad first impression.

I come across another spiral staircase and begin walking up to it until I hear my name being yelled.

"Annalise!" Harvey shouts, grabbing my attention.

"Yeah?" I reply.

His voice is panicky. Afraid. "Don't go up there!"

"Why not?"

I slowly begin to walk down and he visibly relaxes.

"That's where our family business operates from at home. No children allowed." He explains.

I'm about to protest and tell him how I'm not a child but he talks before I can get any words out.

"Wanna watch a movie now?" He asks hastily.

"Sure." I respond, still slightly confused. I brush the feeling off quickly, though. They don't know me. There's no reason for them to tell me anything. "What movie are we watching?"

"Whatever you want." He says, a soft smile glazing over his lips.

Harvey leads me downstairs and down a narrow hallway. We walk into the cinema room and, like everything else in this house, it's amazing. There's a huge screen, just like a real cinema, and it even has the same seats.

I'm lead to a shelf full of CD's, and I pick a random one. Harvey sets it up and we sit in the best spot: middle row, middle seats.

The door opens and the loud sound ricochets off of the walls.

A young looking—but still intimidating—boy walks in. His hair is blonde, his eyes are light brown.

"Hey, Lijah." Harvey says. "Wanna watch the movie with us?" He asks. I offer a small smile to Elijah, who I remember being told was the youngest of my brothers, and he returns it.

"Sure." He responds, walking over and sitting on the other side of me.

————

My dad punches my cheek, the ring on his finger making it hurt even more. I try to scream, but my throat is closed up. I can't talk. I can't shout. I can't beg for him to stop.

I'm defenceless.

"You stupid little bitch!" He exclaims, pushing me, making me fall. He bends down so that he's on my level and lifts my chin so that I'm forced to look at him, to meet the eyes that once belonged to my kind, loving father but have been passed down the abusive shell of the man he used to be.

"I wish you were dead and not Jessie. She made me happy. You make me miserable." He tells me, the scent of alcohol lingering in his breath, shooting out at me with each word he slurs over.

He grabs my hair and pulls me up, he takes me over to the stairs and shoves me. Each step makes my body ache more and more. I hit the last step, landing on my arm, and let out a loud cry. I clutch onto where it hurts, which only makes it hurt more.

I feel my arms being restrained and clench my eyes shut. The more I struggle, the more the grip on my arms tighten.

"Please.." I choke out, tears mixing with the blood from where dad punched me.

"Annalise!" A voice that isn't my fathers shouts. "Wake up!"

"Please don't hurt me.." I whisper.

And then, my eyes shoot open, revealing Elijah and Harvey.. and the rest of my brothers.

chapter three - deception

- -

I feel like a piece of art on display as all seven of my brothers watch me, awaiting an explanation. I sink back into my seat, wishing more than anything that it could just swallow me whole so that I can avoid this conversation.

"Anna—" Harvey begins, but he's quickly cut off by an angry voice.

"What the fuck was that!" Jameson—I think—yells.

I look at each of my brothers and match them up to the pictures I was shown. When my gaze finally lands on Archie, my oldest brother and temporary guardian, I can't help but be scared when his piercing gaze meets my own.

"I get nightmares sometimes.. it's not a big deal. Sorry for worrying you." I say, trying to get up but Elijah pulls me back down from my arm. My left arm. It takes everything in me not to shove his hand away and whimper in pain.

"That was not a nightmare, that was a fucking seizure!" Grayson shouts, grabbing everybody's attention.

All of my brothers begin arguing—apart from Elijah, he draws small circles with his thumb where his hand is still holding my arm. I look over at him, and he gives me a sympathetic smile.

I hate those.

I look down at my lap, then back up again. It's only dawned on me now that this was the first impression I had with most of my brothers. I clench my eyes shut out of embarrassment. All of my brothers just watched me have a nightmare about my abusive dad. Well, our abusive dad, I suppose.

"Shut up!" Archie shouts, shutting everybody up. His voice is commanding, stern, and not at all brotherly. It's the type of voice that can make a whole room of people be quiet. He turns to me, an eyebrow raised. "Well?"

"It was just a nightmare." I mumble, afraid of my eldest brothers stare.

He crosses his arms, a small warning that he could be here all day, and leans on the back of the chair in front of me. "The truth, please."

"That was the truth." I respond defensively.

"Stop lying!" Cole shouts, and he shuts up with one warning look from Archie.

"Annalise." Harvey says from beside me. "That wasn't just a nightmare. You were terrified. What happened?"

Oh, I had a flashback from when my dad pushed me, his own daughter, down the stairs. "I can't remember." I lie.

"Bullshit!" Jameson exclaims, running a hand through his brown hair. He looks over to Archie. "Do you believe this?"

My oldest brother looks at me. Normally, I can tell what people are feeling with their body language and facial expressions. But I can't with Archie, he hides his emotions perfectly. It's almost infuriating.

"I think that when Annalise is ready to tell us the truth, she will." He says. "Or we'll find out on our own. We always do."

He looked at Jameson while saying that, but I know it was directed at me. Archie walks out, and slowly, one by one, everybody else follows until it's only Harvey, Elijah and I left. They both look at each other with concern, then back at me.

"Wanna get some food?" Elijah asks.

I look over at him, and a half-smile appears on my face. "Sure."

————

We get into the kitchen and I sit at the dining table across from Elijah while Harvey goes into the kitchen. He said he'd make sandwiches.

"You okay?" Elijah inquires.

I furrow my eyebrows for a moment, thinking over it.

"I think so." I respond honestly. He looks at me for a few seconds, and I'm confused how he, and all of my other brothers, can just stare at somebody that long without bursting into laughter.

As he's about to say something, Harvey walks in. I silently thank him for interrupting whatever Elijah was about to say; I don't think I can talk about my feelings for any longer.

Harvey sets a sandwich with multiple garnishes in front of me and I can't help but drool. It looks amazing.

"Our chefs are on holiday, so these are leftover sandwiches from when Cole cooked yesterday." He explains, passing me a fork.

"Thanks." I smile. I look down at the appealing food and my stomach churns. I haven't been able to eat anything without throwing it back up a few hours later in a few days. So, as much as I want to eat every last bite of this food, I can't.

"Anna?" Harvey says, snapping me out of my small trance and into the present. "What's wrong?"

I can feel my palms become sweaty and my head begins to ache.

"Nothing.." I mumble, picking up the fork and taking a bite out of the delicious food.

————

I run to the bathroom linked with my bedroom and kneel in front of the toilet, throwing up today's dinner.

"Anna?" Someone says. I can't make out their voice. "Shit, Leo!"

Two sets of footsteps run over to me and somebody pulls my hair back, out of my face.

A glass of water is put up to my lips once I'm finished, and I take it with trembling hands. I don't realise I've drank the whole thing until somebody takes it from me to refill it.

I blink a few times, clearing my glassy eyes and sending a few tears down my cheeks. That's when I see Elijah and Leo kneeling next to me, concern visible on both of their faces.

"Fuck—Anna are you okay?" Elijah asks, breaking the silence. He puts the back of his hand on my forehead, making me flinch but he doesn't notice, thankfully. Or, if he does, he doesn't mention it, which I'm grateful for. "You're burning up."

"Come on, let's get you to bed." Leo says, taking my hand and pulling me up from the cold, tiled floor.

As we walk out of the bathroom, Leo doesn't let go out of my hand, the small action making my heart warm.

A/N: there are gonna be a few mental/physical illnesses in this book, so if I write

chapter four - blamed

I'm woken up by somebody tapping lightly on my shoulder.

I flutter my eyes open and blink a few times, adjusting them to the bright light shining through the blinds. I smile. That was the best sleep I've in a long time.

"How you feeling?" Leo asks, setting a short glass of water onto the wooden beside table and sitting next to me, making the bed dip.

"I feel fine. Thanks." I tell him, picking up the glass of water and sipping it, the coolness of the liquid calming my throat.

He looks down for a moment, and then back up at me. As he's about to say something, his phone dings with a text. He reluctantly takes it out of his pocket, signing.

"Archie wants to speak to you." He tells me. "Come on, I'll take you to his office."

He stands up, and so do I. As we walk out of my room, I tie my hair into a low ponytail with a black bobble on my wrist.

I can't help but feel out of place here in my old pyjamas and white, fluffy socks whilst almost all of my brothers dress prestigiously in their suits and expensive clothes. I'm the black sheep of the family, no matter how much I try to deny it. I don't know if I'll ever really be a part of their family.

We reach a door and Leo knocks on it twice.

"Come in." A voice from inside shouts.

Leo opens the door, revealing a medium-sized, darkly decorated room. The walls are painted dark grey and the back wall is lined with dark oak bookshelves. In the middle of the room is a desk covered in stacks of paper, and behind said desk is my oldest brother.

Archie looks behind me at Leo and nods, and a few moments later the door shuts, leaving me with my most scariest brother.

I look at one of the two chairs on the other side of his desk, and then back at him. I see something close to amusement dance in his eyes; probably at my nervousness.

"You can sit." He tells me, a small smile creeping up on his lips, however it disappears as quickly as it came, and is replaced with a stern straight line.

I slowly walk over to the chair and sit down, setting my hands on my lap.

"I'm sorry I haven't been able to talk to you yet." He says. "I've had things in work that I've needed to prioritise."

Prioritise over the sister you haven't seen since she was two? I want to ask, however I refrain from it.

"It's okay." I tell him, smiling softly.

There's silence for a moment as he just looks at me, like he can't believe I'm really here.

"You were sick last night?" He says, turning the statement into more of a question as though he needs me to confirm it.

"Uh—yeah. I'm fine now, though." I quickly reply.

"That's good to hear." He tells me, smiling a small smile. "Though if it ever happens again I expect you to find one of us after, okay?"

I nod.

"Please use your words, Annalise. So that I can ensure you understand what I'm saying." He requests.

"Oh, alright. Yeah, I'll get someone if I throw up again." I assure him.

"Good. Now, we have rules that you'll be expected to follow." He tells me.

Rules?!

"Okay.." I reply shortly.

"1. We don't tolerate sass, swearing, rudeness or attitude. 2. If me or another one of your brothers tell you do do something, we expect you to do it. It'll be in your best interest. 3. Don't leave the house without permission off of somebody, and if you are allowed to go, we need to know where you're going. 4. No boys. 5. Your grades don't have to be perfect, but we expect you to try your best in school. You will not have a bedtime, but I advise you try to get at least eight hours of sleep. We eat meals together three times a week, but for the other four days you can eat when you want, three times a day." He explains sternly. "Is that all understood?"

"Yes." I respond, remembering he prefers me to use my words.

"Okay." He says. "Is there anything you think I should know?"

"No." I reply.

"Alright, you may go." He tells me.

My heart aches for a moment. He didn't want to see me to be big brotherly, he wanted to see me in order to explain their family rules, to ensure I don't ruin their reputation.

I stand up and walk over to the door, muttering a quick 'bye' as I make my way out into the narrow hallway, shutting the door behind me. Once I make sure I'm alone, I release a breath I didn't know I was holding.

————

My door suddenly opens, the loud noise startling me, and Jameson storms in, anger clear on his red face.

"Where the fuck is it, Annalise?" He shouts, walking closer to me.

"Wheres what?" I question, my throat closing up, just like it does when I'm about to cry.

"Do you think I'm fucking stupid? Where's my weed, Annalise? I know you took it." He yells, his voice making me flinch.

"Why would I take your weed?" I question.

"Whats with all the yelling?" Cole asks, walking in calmly.

"This little bitch took my weed." Jameson answers, pointing at me.

Cole looks at me, an eyebrow raised. Then, he turns back to his brother. He crosses his arms over his chest. "She didn't take it, Jamie. I saw Elijah go into your room."

"Did someone say my name?" Elijah inquires, strolling in. Are we having a family meeting inside my bedroom?

"Did you take my weed?" Jameson asks him, getting straight to the point.

"Oh, yeah, sorry. I meant to give it back." His twin informs him, clearly as high as a kite.

From the corner of my eye, I see Jameson look back at me, and I swear I see guilt flash through his eyes, however he turns away too quickly for me to identify it. He walks back out, mumbling something to Elijah before he reaches the door.

Is this what all of my brothers think of me? That I'm some untrustworthy kid who's so desperate to get high that she'd steal her brothers weed? I don't blame them, to be honest. I'm a random girl who came into their house from a poorer family, and now lives with them. I wouldn't be surprised if they've locked away all of the expensive silverware.

I stand up and walk over to my bathroom, ignoring Elijah saying my name. I turn the shower on and quickly rip my clothes off before stepping in.

chapter five - dear diary

I tie my damp hair into a ponytail and sigh, staring into the small mirror that sits upon my desk. I hum a quiet tune to myself and get out the diary I brought from the duffel bag that still sits under my bed, full of clothes, along with a pen.

I sit down on my bed and open up the notebook, flicking to an empty page. When I find one, I begin writing.

Dear Diary,

I don't know what, or how, to feel. About any of this. When I was told I have brothers who are going to take me in, I was ecstatic. I thought I was going to have a proper family. But boy was I wrong.

Jameson blamed me for taking his stupid weed. And that had me thinking, do all of my brothers see me as some drug-taking kid? Probably.

I'm about to write more when my door opens. I quickly shut the turquoise-coloured notepad and look up, seeing Elijah standing in my doorway, his arms crossed over his chest, and a suspicious—yet also amused—expression on his face.

"What're you hiding?" He asks, walking over.

"Nothing," I respond, smiling innocently.

He glares at me playfully, as though he's trying to figure me out, but eventually gives in when I don't fold.

"Hm, okay." He says, sitting on the end of my bed awkwardly. I look down at the sheet covering my mattress until he talks again. "Annalise."

I snap my head up at the sound of my name. Elijah's eyes are soft. Sad, almost.

"Yeah?" I reply.

He inhales and runs a hand through his blonde hair. Elijah looks up to the ceiling, then back at me, almost as if he's readying himself. For what? I don't know.

"We're all still getting used to having you here." He begins, the small smile left on my face is replaced by a straight line. He makes eye contact with me and his light brown eyes immediately widen. "Not that we don't like having you here, we do, we're all glad you're home."

Home. I think I could get used to that.

"But some of us—like Jameson—are still getting used to it." He sees my confused face and sighs. "What I'm trying to say is, ignore Jameson and him accusing you of stealing his stuff. He's being immature and stupid. He just needs more time to accept the fact that you're really here. That's all. And clearly he's not doing that very well."

So he accuses me of stealing his weed because he 'needs more time'? I avoid saying, mainly because I don't want to ruin this peaceful moment.

"That makes no sense." I respond. "I'm not stupid, Elijah. I know that's not the reason he blamed me for stealing his weed."

"Anna—"

"He, and probably all of you, think that I'm some drug-addict, bad behaved kid who's only here to steal your stuff then make a run for it." I say, and I regret the words leaving my mouth as soon as a wave of sadness overcomes Elijah's face. I carry on, anyway, because they need to know this. "I don't wanna stay here if this is what it's gonna be like."

"Jameson didn't—" He starts to say, but I cut him off again.

"And why are you apologising for him anyway? If he wants to say sorry so badly, I'm sure he can say it himself rather than sending somebody to do it on his behalf." I interrupt, anger washing over me.

Elijah closes his eyes and only opens them when he's composed himself. He turns to me, his eyes pleading. He's about to say something when he's cut off. But not by me.

"What's going on?" Harvey asks, letting himself in.

"Annalise thinks that we think she's a drug addict and a thief." Elijah answers, and my mouth widens while his turns into a satisfied smirk.

"That isn't what I said!" I shout, feeling a need to defend myself.

Amusement plays on Elijah's face as he looks back at me, I only cross my arms and lean back on the headboard of my bed in annoyance.

"It is." Elijah argues, more seriously this time.

I glare at him, and he tries to suppress a laugh but fails.

"Is that a glare?" He inquires, narrowing his eyes, though I can tell by the way the corners of his mouth are lifting upwards he's only teasing.

"Yes. Yes it is." I say.

"Who are you trying to intimidate with that? The wallpaper?" He asks. I hear Harvey chuckle from his place in my room.

I kick Elijah lightly with my foot and he fakes a frown.

"That hurt." He lies.

"Yeah, sure it did." I counter.

"I just came to tell you that dinners ready." Harvey interrupts, smirking.

My smile drops, and I look down.

"I'm not really hungry." I tell, biting my lip slightly out of nervousness.

"Why not?" Harvey inquires.

"My stomach kinda hurts." I respond, and it isn't entirely a lie.

Harvey and Elijah share a concerned look before returning their attention to me again. My throat clenches from fear that they won't believe my lie and I'll throw up at the dinner table. In front of everybody. And then my fresh start will be ruined.

Elijah rests his hand on my upper arm and I wince from the pain his touch causes on the bruise. His eyebrows furrow I'm confusion and I quickly move my arm away from him.

"What's up with your arm?" He asks, tilting his head.

"Nothing." I assure him hastily.

"Oh really?" He says. I nod. "Alright then, lift up your sleeve."

I look between him and Harvey before lifting up my right sleeve.

"Your other sleeve, Annalise." Elijah demands, his voice stern.

"No."

"Yes."

"No."

"Oh for fucks sake, Anna." Harvey says, grabbing my arm and lifting my left sleeve up. I hear his breathing hitch and look away, not wanting to see their reactions.

The secret I've been doing my best to keep is out.

"Holy shit!" A voice that isn't Harvey, nor Elijah's shouts. My head snaps toward the door and standing there is a stumbling Grayson. He's clearly drunk. "What happened to you?" He asks, slurring over his words.

"That's none of your business." I respond, going to pull my sleeve down but Harvey grabs my hand before I can and shakes his head, a silent warning.

"Can you guys hurry the—holy shit!" Somebody else says, storming in. I shut my eyes, annoyed. Why is everybody coming into my room? I look up and see Cole, staring intensely at the purple bruise that covers the majority of my arm, like if he looks at it hard enough it'll magically disappear. If only that was the case.

Now, Harvey, Elijah, Cole and Grayson are all looking at me, waiting for an answer. An explanation. An explanation that I'm too afraid to give.

"Are you just gonna sit there and wait for your arm to grow a fucking mouth and explain why half your arm is goddam purple or are you going to tell us yourself?" Cole inquires angrily. Although I have a feeling that his anger isn't directed at me.

"It's fine." I say, and try to get up from the bed but Grayson places a hand on my shoulder and easily pushes me back down. This whole thing seems to have sobered him up a little bit.

"It's definitely not fine. You have a massive bruise on your arm." Elijah says.

There's silence as they all wait for me to speak.

"Fine, if you won't answer us you can answer Archie instead." Cole warns, pulling out his phone and scrolling until he shows me the screen, hovering his thumb over the call button under my oldest brothers name.

"I fell, that's all." I lie after a few moments, intimidated by their stares.

"Tell the truth, bambina." Harvey whispers from beside me. It's only now I realise he's holding my hand in his, rubbing his thumb over the back of it gently.

I switch my gaze between my brothers and sigh. There's no way I'm getting out of this.

A/N: sorry for the slight cliff-hanger, I guess you'll just have to add this to your library and wait until the next chapter comes out :)

Please vote, comment and feel free to leave any suggestions. Thank you for reading! It means the world to me <3

Word count: 1424.

chapter six - truth

I look at the empty doorway before jumping off of my bed and making a run for it. As I sprint down the hallway, I hear footsteps close behind, but block the sound out.

It doesn't take me long to realise that this was a stupid thing to do. I live with these guys, so it'll be extremely hard to avoid them. But I can try to for as long as I can. And I most definitely will try.

"Annalise!" Harvey's voice echos through the halls, and it only makes me pick up my pace. "Annalise!" He repeats, his voice a mix of anger, sadness and concern. Angry because I ran away. Sad because I'm shutting them out. And concerned because of the bruise that has ruined everything.

I turn a corner and bump into a wall. Oops. Not a wall. Leo. I try to get around him but he blocks me.

"Where are you running to?" He asks, stretching his arm out so I can't walk past him.

"Me and Harvey are playing tag. Please move before he gets me." I lie, faking an innocent smile.

"Okay, but hurry up and finish your game because dinner's probably getting cold." He responds, I nod.

He moves his arm and I immediately begin to run once again, shooting him a thankful smile before he walks away.

Leo's POV:

She runs away, crazy girl. I laugh a small laugh to myself before Harvey, Elijah, Cole and Grayson come running around the same corner Annalise just did.

"Did Anna go this way?" Elijah asks, out of breath.

"Yeah, she said you guys are playing tag. Four on one isn't very fair you know." I respond, and they furrow their eyebrows in confusion.

"We're not playing tag, bro. She has a massive fucking bruise on her arm and ran away when we tried to get her to tell us how she got it." Cole explains.

"Holy shit." I mumble, my eyes widening. I look up at my younger brothers who are just staring at me. "Well let's fucking find her then! Idioti!" (T: idioti-idiots)

All five of us run down the hall, shouting Annalise's name until eventually we see her sitting inside the open library, hugging her knees to her chest. A small sob escapes her lips and my heart breaks into a thousand pieces.

"Fuck—Anna.." I whisper, walking over to her. I kneel so that I'm closer to her level and wrap my arms around her. I release a small breath I didn't know I was holding when I feel her hands connect behind my back.

I've waited so long for the moment I get to hug my little sister again. And that time has finally come.

"I'm sorry." She mumbles, her voice shaking.

I pull away and wipe a stray tear dripping down her cheek. "For what?" I ask softly.

"For running away." She responds, her bottom lip wiggling a little bit. "And not telling you why there's a bruise on my arm."

"It's alright, sweetheart." I assure her, my voice coming out as a whisper. After a few more short seconds of silence, I say, "can I see the bruise?"

She wipes her nose, sniffling, and them pulls her left sleeve up, revealing a huge, purple bruise running up her entire arm. A small gasp leaves my mouth, and she looks away, almost as if she's ashamed.

I tilt her head toward me with my pointer finger.

"How did you get that bruise, Annalise?" I inquire, she stiffens. "You can tell me." I assure her quietly.

"M-my dad pushed me down the stairs." She answers quickly, then looks down at the marble floor, breathing in and out.

Annalise's POV:

As soon as the words leave my mouth, I feel as though a weight has just been lifted off of my shoulders. The secret I've been doing my best to keep is out.

I look up, past Leo, past Harvey, Grayson, Cole and Elijah and at Archie, who must've gotten here while I wasn't looking. His fists are clenched to his sides, and his nostrils are slightly flared in anger.

Leo's gentle squeeze on my hand makes me look at him again. He puts a comforting smile on, something that hardly helps hide the anger clear in his eyes.

"Did he do anything else to you, Anna?" My second oldest brother asks.

I sigh and turn my body, lifting up my shirt and allowing the marks my fathers belt left to be shown. I clench my eyes shut, trying so desperately not to cry more than I already have.

"Fucking hell." Cole mumbles, loud enough for me to hear. "Leo, her spine is literally sticking out."

Leo shoots him a harsh glare, silently warning him to shut up, which I'm grateful for. He didn't have to word it like that, but he's right. My spine sticks out of my back like a sore thumb.

Leo pieces everything together and sighs.

"That's why you threw up?" He questions.

"Yeah.." I respond quietly, refusing to meet his eyes. When I finally do, I decide to elaborate. "He wouldn't let me eat anything for random days at a time. One day, when I was allowed to again, I threw up straight after. That was about two weeks ago."

"You haven't ate properly in over two weeks?" Elijah cuts in. I shake my head no and his eyes widen slightly. "We need to take you to the hospital, then!" He exclaims, looking at his brothers. Cole nods his head in agreement, Grayson stumbles over himself, Harvey looks down at the floor and Archie clenches his jaw.

I don't know where Jameson is, but I'm glad he's not here in case he accuses me of stealing something else.

"We'll take her tomorrow." Archie speaks, his voice commanding. It's the first thing he's said since he arrived. I open my mouth, ready to object, but my eldest brother beats me to it. "It's not up for discussion."

And with that, he leaves. Slowly, one by one, all of my brothers filter out, just like they did in the cinema room. They even give me the same, sympathetic smiles.

"Come on, let's get you some soup or something." Leo smiles, standing up and reaching his hand out to me. I take it, scrambling to my feet, and he doesn't let go of my hand as we walk out of the library.

A/N: sorry this chapter is quite short, and I'm also sorry for uploading it quite late. I had a netball tournament thing that lasted a while so I couldn't work on this for a long time.

Anyways, I hope that you guys are happy with this chapter.

Word count: 1126.

chapter seven - red apples

- -

E lijah hands me a bowl of a greenish-brownish coloured soup and a spoon. I nervously take a small bite of the liquid, then shove the spoon into my mouth and swallow it quickly. I wait a few seconds, and when I don't feel like I'm going to throw up, I eat more. And more. Until the bowl is eventually empty.

For the first time in a long time, I feel full.

...Until I feel something stuck inside my throat. I widen my eyes and run over to the sink, making it just in time so that I can throw up in it.

A strong hand rubs circles on my back as I hover over the metal sink, readying myself in case more of my swallowed food decides to make an appearance.

"It's okay.." Elijah whispers softly, wrapping his arms around my shoulders comfortingly. I can't help but melt into his warm embrace. He turns me around and pulls me into his chest, hugging me. I wish that I could capture this moment with a picture and frame it, despite the sad reasoning behind it.

From the corner of my eye, I see Leo walk in. He drops whatever is in his hands onto the marble countertop and rushes over to us, joining in on the hug.

"Group hug." Elijah mumbles, I laugh, so does Leo.

This feels nice. Knowing that I have people who care about me—even if it's only a little bit—makes me happy. It's all I've ever wanted.

"Come on, let's go and watch a movie." Elijah says, taking my hand and walking out of the kitchen, giving me no time to respond—or even react.

I struggle to keep up with his fast-paced walking, which he notices and only quickens it, a small, proud smirk on his face. When we eventually get to the cinema room, I'm close to being out of breath.

"You're a fast walker." I complain.

"Or you're just slow." He winks, and then laughs when I glare at him again. "You should really work on that glare, princess."

I cross my arms over my chest, only making him laugh more. To me, I think I look pretty badass right now, but I probably look like a small puppy who's trying to be intimidating to him.

I roll my eyes and as I go to walk to one of the cinema seats, he pulls me back. "Don't roll your eyes at me, you little baby." He warns.

"I'm not a baby." I respond.

"Yes you are." He counters.

"No, I'm not." I say, frustrated.

"You are." He tells me.

"No."

"Yes."

"No."

"Yes."

He stares at me, the same way Harvey did the first time I met him, though Elijah isn't trying to find out all of my secrets, he's trying to intimidate me. And it's kinda working. I feel very small under his intense stare.

"Can you stop?" I ask, my voice coming out shaky.

"Stop what?" He responds, acting oblivious.

"Looking at me like that." I say.

"Am I not allowed to look at you?" He inquires, furrowing his eyebrows. I can see amusement dancing in his eyes.

"I didn't say that." I reply.

"What did you say then?" He asks.

He's pissing me off.

"You're looking at me like you're about to shoot me, Elijah." I tell him, and I swear I see him stiffen at my words.

"I'm not going to shoot you." He says shortly.

"Good. Because that would be mean." I respond.

We just stand there in an awkward silence, both of us waiting for the other to say something, until the door opens, and in walks a man who I've never seen before. His hair is dark brown, and he has a beard the same colour. I can't make out the colours of his eyes in the dimly-lit room, however I can make out that he's out of breath.

"Elijah.." He says, panting for more air. "You—you're needed..up stairs."

They share a knowing look, and Elijah turns to me. The other man looks to me too, and raises his eyebrows, surprised that I'm here. He ran in so fast I'm not sure he saw me.

"How about we watch a movie later, yeah?" Elijah asks, smiling softly.

I look between my brother and the mysterious man. "Uh.. sure."

"Okay, great." Elijah says, patting me on the shoulder and running out with the man. He glances back at me and offers a small smile. One that I return.

————

"You useless little bitch!" My father spits. I regain my balance, and he only pushes me back down again.

"I'm sorry.." I whisper, tears rolling down my face.

He kneels down to my level, and I can smell the alcohol in his breath as he talks.

"What'd you just say?" He asks, grabbing my chin and forcing me to meet his eyes. The eyes of a man who used to be my father. My best friend.

"I'm sorry." I repeat.

"Good. You should be." He tells me angrily. He stands back up again and swings his foot forward, right into my face.

I let out a cry, holding the spot he hurt, so much blood is pouring on my hand that I'm sure it'll leave some kind of stain.

My dad pulls me up by my hair and pins me to the wall. He punches me one. Two. Three. Three times. How could a father do this to their child?

"Annalise!" A voice that isn't my fathers yells.

"My life would be been so much better if you weren't in it." He tells me.

"Anna!" The voice says again. My eyes snap open. I frantically look around, trying to figure out where I am, and it doesn't take me long to recognise my bedroom. I'm laying on my bed, a blanket half-on me, in Harvey's arms.

"Shhhh, you're okay, bambina." He whispers assuringly, not letting go of me. Which is something I'm grateful for. Being wrapped in his arms makes me feel safe, safer than I've ever felt. "It's okay.." Harvey tells me quietly.

I blink the tears out of my eyes and steady my breathing. I tilt my head back slightly and look at a very concerned Harvey. His eyebrows are furrowed and his eyes are searching my face as though he's looking for something.

"What happened, Annalise?" He asks softly.

I have to bite my bottom lip to keep it from trembling.

I look at Harvey who's so desperate for answers. Who's so desperate to help. But the last time I let somebody in, they left just as quickly as they came, taking my ability to trust easily with them.

"It's fine.." I dismiss, "you didn't have to come in here. The nightmare would have passed. They always do."

He raises en eyebrow. "You have nightmares a lot?"

I shrug with one shoulder, "yeah."

"What are they about?" He questions, looking down at me. I move so that I'm sitting across from him. Harvey leans his head against the headboard of my bed as he awaits my answer.

"Uh—you know.. dinosaurs." I blurt, regretting the lie as soon as I tell it.

Couldn't I have thought of anything better than dinosaurs?

"Dinosaurs?" He repeats, and his lips turn upward into an amused smirk. I nod. "Okay.. what do these dinosaurs do?"

He tilts his head, watching me as I try to come up with something.

"They like.. eat people and stuff." I tell him, and his smile grows wider. "It's not funny! It's very traumatising."

He nods and looks down. When he looks up at me again, his eyes are softer. Calmer. Like he, for a moment, jumped into my mind and understands everything.

"Please don't lie to me, Annalise." He pleads.

The majority of my brothers have a nickname for me. So when they call me Annalise, it makes me feel as though I'm in trouble. I know Harvey doesn't mean to make me feel like I've done something wrong, but I still do nevertheless.

I inhale slowly. "It was about my dad hitting me. Not that what I dream about is any of your business." I mumble the last part, but he still hears it.

"I'm only trying to—" He begins, but I cut him off.

"Help?" I assume, "yeah, I know."

I feel guilty as I watch his eyes drop, but if my brothers want me to talk about my feelings, then I suppose that it's time I do.

"What's with the attitude, Annalise?" Harvey asks.

"What's with the knowing I existed for eleven years and not making any move to try and find me, Harvey?" I mock, and he stiffens. When the words leave my mouth, I really think about it. I think about how they knew who I was yet didn't try to find out where I was. Not once. They couldn't messaged me. Called me. Even messaged me on Instagram and I would've been happy.

"Not even a phone call." I mumble to myself, scoffing and rolling my eyes after.

A new thought comes into my head.

Imagine all the stuff I wouldn't have had to have gone through if they would've just looked for me the day dad took me.

"Annalise.." Harvey says. He takes a deep breath before continuing. "We tried to find you, believe me. There wasn't a day that went by where somebody didn't mention your name. Even if it was something small. Like once we were eating lunch, a fruit salad, and we started a conversation about what fucking fruit we thought would be your favourite." He shakes his head at the thought, a small smile on his lips at the memory.

I furrow my eyebrows. Then, after a few seconds of silence, I talk.

"What'd you decide on?" I ask, he snaps his head toward me.

"Strawberries." He tells me.

"I like strawberries. I prefer apples, though. But they have to be red." I respond.

He smiles at me, and I smile back. I forget about everything I was mad about. Because I doubt they could control it. I mean, my dad probably did all that he could so that I'd never be found.

A/N: this chapters a bit longer, I hope you like it!

Q: which brother is your favourite so far?

Ohmygodwehit100views!

Thank you so much for reading! As always, any votes and comments are highly appreciated!

Word count: 1745.

chapter 8 - crash

After my rather awkward conversation with Harvey ended, I learnt that it's 6:07pm. I must've fallen asleep after coming up from the cinema room.

I make my way down the spiral stairs and into the living room. But I stop in the doorway when I see Elijah sitting on the couch. With a girl. I widen my eyes and pivot on one foot, and I think I've gotten away until my brother calls my name.

"Anna!" He exclaims. I turn back around, and the girl he's with is now facing me. She has long, dark brown hair and her face is heavily made up. Her lipstick is smudged, and that's when I notice how Elijah's lips have reddened. Ew.

"Yeah?" I ask.

"This is.." Elijah looks over at her, "Emma—"

"Ella." She corrects sternly.

Elijah invited her to the house without even knowing her name?

"Oh, right." He says, like her name isn't important. "This is my little sister, Annalise."

I never thought that my name and sister would be in the same sentence. I've always wanted brothers, so this is very surreal to me. I almost can't believe it.

"Hi." I say awkwardly.

"Hey, do you mind getting me some water?" She asks, I furrow my eyebrows. I look over to Elijah, and he has the same expression as me on his face.

I sigh, "sure."

I smirk when my back is turned.

Once I'm in the kitchen, I fill up a tall glass with water and then begin to walk back into the living room.

I walk over to the couch and accidentally spill it all over her short white dress. I hear Elijah stifle a laugh.

"I am so sorry!" I exclaim, and she stands up, looking down at the damage. "Hey, the dress isn't that nice anyway." I try to console her, however it only makes her angrier.

Elijah smirks at me.

"You little brat!" She shouts, and then turns to my brother, expecting him to tell me off. When he doesn't say a word, she speaks again. "Are you just gonna sit there and let your bitch of a sister treat me like this?"

Elijah's eyes darken at her words. He stands up and gets in her face, whispering something that I can't hear. Her eyes widen and she grabs her bag from the floor, running out. She glances back at me and glares. I glare back.

Once we hear the faint sound of the door slamming shut, Elijah bursts out laughing.

"Thank you. She wouldn't leave." He says in between giggles.

I look down, and then up again, a fake smile plastered onto my face. "Yeah. It's fine."

"What's wrong?" He asks.

You promised that you'd watch a movie with me after you finished whatever you had to do. But you were with a girl instead. I don't say, because I get that they can't hang out with me 24/7 and that they have lives. It still hurts, though, that somebody with a name who he couldn't even remember is prioritised over me. Someone he promised.

"Nothing." I assure him before leaving.

I can't help but feel like I'm being dramatic. Elijah has his own life, and I shouldn't be getting in the way of that. Besides, everybody forgets stuff, and we can always watch a movie another day.

While I'm walking back upstairs, Leo calls my name.

"We're going to the beach, get ready!" He orders, and then walks off, giving me no time to respond.

I'm excited to go to the beach, though. I love the feeling when sand is in between your toes and the waves crashing against your legs when you stand in the ocean.

————

We took two separate cars. Elijah, Harvey, Jameson and I are in one and Archie, Leo, Cole and Grayson are in the other. I'm in the backseat with Elijah, and Jameson and Harvey are in the front.

A black car has been following us the entire ride, and Harvey keeps looking back at it in the mirror and then looking at Jameson worriedly.

Within the blink of an eye, the car pulls up next to us and gets too close. It hits our side, over and over again, and I look at Elijah, my eyes wide. He clutches onto my hand so tightly that I'm afraid he's going to rip it off. He won't look at me, though.

Then, our car is pushed off of the road. I hit my head on the back of my seat and my eyelids suddenly become heavy.

"Anna!" Elijah exclaims, taking his seatbelt off. He crawls over to me, his face covered in blood. He takes my belt off, too, and cradles me in his arms. "Keep your eyes open, Anna, please."

I want to, I want to so badly but I can't. I start to see dots and then everything suddenly goes black.

————

Harvey's POV:

I pace around the hospital room, looking at Annalise the whole time. So many wires are connected to her. There are all sorts of needles in her arms, and she even has a feeding tube.

She's been in a coma for two days, and I'm ducking terrified. What if she doesn't wake up? I sit in the seat next to her and put my head in my hands, my breathing heavy and quick. We're all okay, we have a few injuries, like Grayson's broken arm from the way he landed when Archie's car was pushed off the road.

The door opens and Leo walks in, along with Jameson and Elijah. They have food in their hands, but I'm not hungry.

They offer me a plate of hospital food, but I say no.

"Come on, Harvey. You need to have something." Leo tells me, putting the plate on my lap.

The others are at home, trying to find the assholes who crashed into us. They drove away too quickly after shooting at us. We know it was one of our rivals, but we're unsure of which Mafia would be dumb enough to attack us.

Yeah, we're in the Italian Mafia, Archie owns it.

"I'm not hungry." I respond.

"You haven't eaten since the crash." Elijah says.

"That's because I haven't been hungry since the crash." I reply.

"Annalise wouldn't like it if you weren't eating because of her." Leo tells me, I scoff. Did he really just say that?

"Don't start all that shit." I say angrily, standing up.

Annalise's POV:

My eyes flutter open, and the bright light makes my head hurt. I sniffle, and three sets of eyes turn to look at me.

"Anna!" Harvey exclaims, running to my side. "Jamie, go and get the nurse!" He orders Jameson, and he quickly obeys. "Lijah, call the others."

A/N: the idea of a car crash just randomly popped into my head when I was writing the chapter. I'm not that good at writing like injuries so sorry about that badly detailed bit.

Omg tysm, for 400 reads! Yesterday we were on 300. Idk what to say I never even thought my story would just get a view!

Word count: 1190.

chapter 9 - Italian

"How do you feel, bambina?" Harvey inquires quietly, holding my hand with both of his. Leo stands next to him, a concerned but also relieved look on his face.

I look around the hospital room, at the tiled ceiling, the needles on a tray, and at myself. My leg is in a cast, and there's a bandage around my arm, on the spot where I fell when I was pushed down the stairs.

My breathing quickens. "It hurts." I choke out, trying to sit up.

"Where hurts?" Harvey asks quickly.

"Everywhere.." I cry, attempting to get more comfortable. It doesn't work. My whole body feels like it's on fire, and my head is aching horribly.

The door opens, and Jameson and Elijah walk in with a doctor. She has a wooden clipboard in one hand, and in the other is a pen.

"How do you feel, Annalise?" She asks, her voice kind.

"Like I've been swimming in lava." I respond honestly.

"We'll give you some pain meds for that in a little bit, once you've woken up more." She tells me. "Now, your brothers told me about

your ED, we'll prescribe some medication to help with digestion."
The doctor takes a deep breath before continuing. She looks at my
brothers nervously. "It's also recommended that you go to therapy.
We've been told about what happened in your past and now with the
car crash, it'll help you a lot."

"No thanks." I respond, using my arms to help me sit up.

"Anna—" Elijah says.

"I'm not going to therapy." I cut him off, avoiding eye contact with
all four of my brothers that are in the room.

I don't want to sit in some too-warm office on a beanbag chair and
talk to somebody who I don't even know about all of my problems.
It's a waste of time and money.

"Well, it doesn't have to be decided now." She speaks, a smile plastered on her face.

I go to say how I already have decided, but the door opens before
I can get my words out, and the rest of my brothers walk in. Archie
enters first, and his lips turn upwards into a soft smile when he sees
me, but it disappears so quickly that I don't know if I imagined it or
not. Next, Grayson comes in, and his arm is in a cast. Lastly, Cole
makes his way inside, and the left side of his face is covered in a light
bruise.

Cole walks over to me and ruffles my hair. "Welcome back, kid."

————

Hospital food tastes like shit.

The nurse gave me medicine to help with digestion, and if I don't
throw up because of my ED, then it'll be from the taste of this food.

"Come on, Annalise. Just have a few more bites." Harvey says.

"It tastes like sh—" Archie raises an eyebrow warningly from the corner of the room, "crap, it tastes like crap."

I blink, and I'm suddenly really tired. I tried to fall asleep a few hours ago, but I couldn't. Though, I think that had something to do with the beeping monitor next to me that supplies all of the needles that are still connected to my arms.

"Don't be dramatic." Harvey responds.

"You have some, then." I counter.

"Okay." He says, and takes the spoon that lays next to the plate. He takes a bite and visibly grimaces. "Yum." He mumbles before grabbing a tissue and spitting the food into it.

"I told you." I say, crossing my arms. "I think they're trying to poison me."

"Don't be silly. It can't be that bad." Cole says from the dark blue seat next to Harvey.

"Oh yeah? Try it." Harvey challenges.

Cole shrugs and takes the spoon confidently. He takes a bite and grabs my last tissue, coughing the food up.

"Okay, that is bad." He admits, pointing at the plate in front of me.

I nod and let my head fall back on the pillow. I want to go home and sleep in my own bed. This one feels like somebody just put a sheet on a bunch of rocks.

"Anna, are you excited to go to school after the summer holidays are over?" Leo asks, breaking the short silence.

I like learning new things, and my last school was okay, it was the other children who made it hell for me. I can only hope that there are nicer people who go to my new school.

"I don't know." I respond shortly. I'm scared to go, but also a bit excited.

"Are you nervous?" Harvey asks, tilting his head.

"Yeah.." I reply.

"Don't be. It'll be fine. Besides, Elijah and Jameson will be there." Leo says.

I'm pretty sure that if Jameson saw me getting bullied, he'd either laugh or join in. I'm guessing he'd choose the latter.

"Yeah, I guess." I mumble, looking down.

The door opens and the doctor walks in. I snap my head towards her with hope. Hopefully they let me go home.

"So, Annalise. We have to keep you another day for observation, but after that you're free to go." She smiles, and I frown.

I have to spend the night in this creepy hospital?

I didn't realise I said that out loud until Cole slaps my hand gently. "Don't be rude." He says, though I can hear the amusement in his voice behind the sternness.

"I didn't mean—" I begin, but the doctor cuts me off.

"It's okay. Hospitals can be creepy." She admits, a smile on her face. "But don't worry, there aren't any ghosts or anything. One of your brothers can stay if you want—they'll be able to sleep in the other bed in the room."

Then, as if on cue, all of my brothers look at me.

"Oh.. uh. No. It's fine. I can stay by myself." I respond.

"Alright. If you change your mind, just let me know," she says, nodding. She leaves the room, making this visit, just like all of her others, short.

Harvey turns to me. "You don't want anybody to stay with you?" He asks, confused.

I shake my head. "No. You have your own lives." I look up from the blanket covering me to find that all of my brothers are staring at me. "Besides, these beds are uncomfortable. I don't think any of you would want to stay here."

"Anna, if you think we don't want to—" Cole starts.

"I didn't say that. Im sure some of you might want to, but I don't need you to. Im not a baby." I whisper the last part.

"Yes you are." Elijah says, and a glare breaks out on my face.

"You can't be mean to me. My leg is broken." I respond.

"It's fractured, not broken." Harvey jumps in.

"Oh. Same thing." I dismiss.

As Harvey goes to correct me, the sound of a phone ringing interrupts him. I look over to Archie, who has a phone to his ear and is quickly going to the corner of the room.

"Li hai già trovati?" Archie says into the phone. My eyebrows immediately furrow in confusion. (T: have you found them yet?)

"Is he speaking Spanish?" I ask Harvey in a whisper, leaning closer to him.

He laughs a short laugh. "No, bambina, he's speaking Italian,"

"He can speak Italian?" I ask, amazed.

"We all can. And soon, you'll be able to, too." He tells me.

"Why?" I ask.

"You're half Italian, Anna." Cole answers.

"Really?"

"Yes." Harvey responds, smirking.

"Non mi interessa. Voglio gli stronzi che pensavano fosse una buona idea darci la caccia, specialmente quando Annalise era con noi, morta." Archie says, his voice coming out like venom. (T: I don't care. I want the assholes who thought it'd be a good idea to come after us, especially when Annalise was with us, dead.)

A/N: Tysm for all the views WHAT. When I first pressed 'add story', I never thought that I'd make it this far, thank you.

Word count: 1342.

chapter 10 - fear

I can't sleep. The monitor is too loud, the room is too cold, and this hospital is even creepier at night than day.

I'm slowly beginning to regret not asking one of my brothers to stay here with me.

I grab the crutches the doctor gave me and carefully get off of the bed. I slowly open the wooden door before making my way out into the eery hallway.

I sit on a cushioned bench and breathe in and out, trying to make myself more tired. A masculine voice snaps me back into reality, and I look up.

A tall, dirty-blonde haired boy stands over me, his eyes are a pale green, and a soft smile grazes his lips. "Can I sit?" He asks.

I move my crutches out of the way of the space next to me and nod. "Sure."

Like me, he's wearing a hospital gown. He clutches onto a monitor much like the one I have in the room I'm staying in.

"What're you here for?" He inquires, looking into my eyes and, for a moment, I'm lost for words.

I debate wether I should tell him the truth or not. It doesn't take me long to conclude that I should, because there isn't anything wrong with the truth.

"I was in a coma for two days, and my leg is fractured." I finally say.

"How come?" He asks.

"Hm?" I respond, confused as to what he's asking.

"I mean why were you in a coma?" He clears his question up, smiling. I smile, too. Because his is contagious.

"Oh. Car crash." I inform him. "What about you?"

"My appendix burst." He tells me. "Why are you awake so late?"

"I can't sleep." I say.

"Oh. I'm waiting for my brother to come back from the vending machine. He went there with his friend and he's taking ages." He explains.

"Mason!"

"Annalise?"

Two voices speak at the exact same time, and my head snaps to the end of the corridor. Archie is standing there, along with somebody who looks like an older version of the boy next to me.

They both walk over to us, and Mason and I look at each other. "You're Annalise?" He asks, raising both of his eyebrows in surprise.

"Yeah?" I reply, confused as to why he's so puzzled.

"What're you doing out of your bed?" Archie asks when he and who I'm assuming to be Masons brother reach us.

"I thought you went home?" I question.

He looks away, then back at me. His eyes soften as he speaks. "Yeah, well, I didn't."

A small smile plants itself on my lips. He didn't leave. Maybe he was waiting for his friend to arrive so that he could keep him company, or maybe he stayed for me. I suppose I'll never know. Though, I like to think it was the second choice.

"Anna, this is Dean." Archie says, motioning towards the man beside him quickly.

"Hey." Dean speaks.

"Hi." I respond.

"Come on, Annalise. Let's get you back to bed." Archie says, getting my crutches that are leaning against the wall and handing them to me. I go to protest, but he quickly shuts me up with the raise of an eyebrow and a warning look. Something that shouldn't be intimidating, yet strangely is.

I slowly stand up, keeping my hand on the white wall as I do so in order to maintain my balance before taking the crutches from Archie and muttering a quick, 'thanks.'

"Goodnight, Annalise." Mason says.

"Goodnight," I respond, smiling.

Archie puts his hand on my back and leads me down the hallway in the direction of my hospital room. Once we're inside it, I throw my crutches onto the floor and jump up onto my bed.

I crawl to the head of my bed, dragging my leg that has the cast on behind me. Archie stands awkwardly in the corner of the room, and when I'm under the covers he goes to leave, but I stop him.

"Archie." I say.

He stops and turns around. "Yes?"

I push all my nerves aside. I didn't realise how scared I would be doing something as simple as asking my oldest brother for something.

"Will you stay with me until I fall asleep?" I ask nervously.

He smiles. Like a genuine, big smile. One that he doesn't wash away.

He walks over silently and sits on the chair next to me. I shut my eyes and he holds my hand after a few moments, rubbing circles with his thumb on my palm.

———

The car flips, and my seatbelt rips in half.

"Get out of the car and run, Annalise." Elijah groans, clutching to his stomach.

"I can't just leave you!" I exclaim.

Elijah coughs, and blood pours out of his mouth. He begins to choke on it, and I try to crawl over to him but I can't.

"Elijah!" I shout as his eyes begin to shut.

The door next to me opens and I expect it to be one of my brothers, but it's a man I don't know. A man I don't know who's holding a gun.

He points it to the space in between my eyes and pulls the trigger. A scream escapes my lips before everything goes black.

My arms are being held strongly by my sides and I try—and fail—to wriggle out of the tight grip I'm being held in.

"Shh.." Somebody whispers in my ear. "It's okay, Anna. It was just a bad dream. It's not real, a stòr." (T: a stor - darling.)

My breathing gradually slows down, and my eyelids quickly become heavy. Before I fall asleep, I feel somebody wrap their arms around me and kiss the top of my head.

————

Archie's POV:

I wake up, and my arm is wrapped around my little sister, pulling her close to me. Her breaths are even, and she looks really peaceful.

"Say cheese." Cole says, and a bright flash follows.

I didn't even know he was here. I look up, and all of my brothers are watching me.

"Really?" I ask.

Cole smirks. "Had to capture the moment. This is probably the first time you've ever been within a meter from her."

"That's not true." I say.

"Yes, it is. You at like you're scared of her." Elijah responds.

Does Annalise think that too? She's my little sister, and I'm extremely happy she's home. I know I haven't talked to her that much, but I'd lay down my life for her. All I want to do is make sure she's happy, and I'll do whatever it takes to reach that goal. I don't want her to think I don't like her or I don't want her with us, because that is the opposite of what I want.

"Oh, before I forget, Dean asked us to tell you to meet him in Masons room. He needs to talk to you." Harvey says.

"Okay." I reply. I look down at Annalise and slowly move off of the bed, careful not to disturb her sleep. I pull my phone out and check the time.

9:16am.

Masons room is only down the hall, so it doesn't take me that long to get there. I knock on the door and walk in, not waiting for permission to enter.

"Hey." Dean says, standing up. He looks back at Mason and then leans closer, whispering. "Can we talk outside?"

"Yeah, sure." I respond, rubbing my eyes, still a bit tired.

"Your dad got out of jail." He tells me.

"Don't call him that." I say, the words coming out more harsh than I meant for them to be. Just because he's blood related, it does not make him my father.

"Sorry." Dean says before continuing. "Anyway, he got out of jail. One of our guys has been following him, like you asked, and he said that he's been going to a lawyers office. We investigated it and.." he drifts off.

"And what?" I ask.

"He wants Annalise back, Arch." He informs me.

I stiffen. She only just got here, she's not leaving. Not again. Not if I have anything to do with it. "Absolutely not."

"You have a good case against him. But you need to make sure Annalise wants to stay with you, because it all comes down to wether she says yes when the judge asks her if she wants to live with you guys."

"Okay." Is all I say before I walk back down to my sisters room.

A/N: oooo! What do you think will happen?

Also, you don't have to, but I made another story! It's called: the girl with baggage, and can be found on my page!

Word count: 1459.

chapter 11 - memory

Annalise's POV:

I get changed into the clothes Harvey brought for me as Archie signs the paperwork that allows me to leave.

I unlock the bathroom door and walk out, the bag that my things were in flung over my shoulder.

Harvey looks up from his phone and smiles at me. "Ready to go?" He asks, "Archie's just getting the prescription for your medicine. We'll get it on the way home."

Home. I smile at the unfamiliar word.

"Okay." I say.

He motions for me to sit beside him and I do. The silence is awkward as I make my way over to the spot on the bed next to him. The crutches slow me down a great deal.

He turns so that his body is facing mine and sighs.

"Why don't you wanna go to therapy, Annalise?" He asks.

Oh, it's not a how-are-you talk, it's a I-think-you're-crazy-so-you-need-to-go-to-therapy talk.

I'm sure he doesn't think I'm crazy, but he clearly thinks I need help, otherwise he wouldn't have just asked me that.

I avoid eye contact with him until he catches my chin and forces me to look at him. "Answer the question, Anna." I lift my gaze up to the ceiling. "Annalise." He says, more sternly this time.

I finally meet his eyes, and he looks at me with concern.

"Why, Anna?" He questions, his voice coming out as a whisper.

The door opens, and I silently thank Elijah who walks through the door.

"Paperwork's done. Let's get out of here." He says, smiling.

I stand up happily and put my crutches on. "Hey." Harvey speaks, grabbing my attention. "This conversation isn't over." He warns, pointing at me.

I quicken my pace, which is still very slow, and I hear him laugh a little bit behind me at my sudden fear.

"Right, let's get going." Leo announces once I'm out the door and standing in the hall, along with the rest of my brothers.

From the corner of my eye, I see Jameson look at me. A small smile appears on his face when our eyes meet, and I smile back. I think that this is the first time Jameson has looked at me without snarling or scowling. I almost can't believe that it really happened.

—————

Harvey carries me up the stairs, cradling me like a baby. He picked me up so effortlessly, as though I weigh not much more than a feather. When he puts me down, I look down both of the hallways.

I forgot where my room is.

I bite my nails nervously. "Uh, Harvey."

"Yeah?" He responds.

My eyes are watering now. I blink away the tears that are threatening to fall. I don't even know why I'm crying.

"I forgot where my room is." I mumble.

I used to know where it is, but when I try to remember I can't. It's like something has blocked my brain.

He looks over and sees my pained face, furrowing his eyebrows.

"Hey, what's wrong?" Harvey asks, a small laugh leaving his lips as he wraps his arm over my shoulder.

"I don't know where my room is." I admit nervously.

I look at each of the doors, begging my brain to remember something. I left and entered that room hundreds of times, but I can't remember which one it is.

Harvey wraps his arm tighter around me, smiling sympathetically. "It's okay, Anna." He turns me toward him and wipes a tear from my face. "Come on, I'll show you." He winks at me and smiles, and I can't help but smile too.

He pats my shoulder and begins walking slowly so that I can keep up with him. We stop in front of a door, and I still don't remember it.

When he opens the door, revealing the room, nothing comes back to me. The close to white walls and the carpeted floor don't ring a bell in my mind.

"Are you sure this is the right room?" I ask nervously.

He laughs a confused, awkward laugh. He looks down at me and his face softens. "Anna.. you don't remember your room?"

I shake my head, and he looks down to the floor.

"Okay. You go in and get some sleep." He says.

I look from him to the door wearily before going inside. The unfamiliar room is cold, and sends a shiver down my spine.

The door shuts behind me, and I jump at the loud sound.

Harvey's POV:

I walk down the stairs and make my way to Archie's office. Anna looked something close to terrified when she had to go into her room.

I knock on the door twice, and I hear Archies muffled 'come in' from the other side.

He's sitting at his desk, doing paperwork.

"What's up?" He asks, looking up at me. I sit on the chair in front of his desk, grabbing his attention more.

"Uh—Annalise. She didn't remember where her room was. Then, when I showed her, thinking that she just, you know, forgot the way or something, she asked me if I was sure it was her room. I think she lost some of her memory, Arch." I explain quickly.

He blinks a few times. "Are you sure?"

"Well, I'm not positive. But she knew where her room is before she went to hospital." I respond. "She remembers important things, but she's clueless about everything else. Like, on the way home, she was just staring at her phone. I asked her what was wrong and she said she forgot her password. I told her I'd help her figure it out. It was 1234, Archie. Nobody forgets a password as simple as that."

"Do you think it's serious?" He inquires. "Like, if we don't get her help then—"

"What do you mean help? Like, medicine?" I question.

As he goes to answer, the sound of somebody pounding on the door cuts him off. We both share a confused look before shooting up from our seats and going to the front door. My mouth drops when I see who's standing there.

"Hello, my sons." He says, a disgusting smile plastered onto his face.

I hear small gasp from the stairs and snap my head toward the sound. Annalise is sitting on one of the steps, tears already rolling down her petrified face.

"The fuck is he doing here?" Cole asks, walking over.

"Ah, Cole. You're so grown up." Benedict smiles. "Now, where's that daughter of mine?"

He tries to walk in, but Archie steps in front of him. "You stay the hell away from her." He demands, his voice leaving like venom.

"Does she know what you guys do?" He asks him, smirking.

"No, and she won't find out." Cole says.

"Won't she?" Benedict asks. There's silence for a moment as the three of us look at him. "Annalise!" He shouts. "Come on, doll, you're coming home with me!"

I look over at the stairs and Annalise isn't there anymore.

When nobody moves, Benedict tries once again to get past Archie, but my brother pins him to the wall. "Both of you go take Anna out for ice cream or something."

Cole and I share a look, and then walk to the stairs. When we reach Anna's room, she's in bed, hugging her knees to her chest and laying on her side. My heart breaks as the sound of her quiet sobs reaches my ears.

Annalise's POV:

"Annalise." Cole says, and I look up, sniffling.

"I don't wanna go with him, you can send me to an orphanage, but not him. Please not him." I plead, and they both walk over.

"Why would we send you to an orphanage, Anna?" Harvey inquires.

"A foster home, then?" I ask.

"You're staying here, Anna." Cole says.

I smile, and another tear falls from my eyes. "Really?"

"You're stuck with us now, Anna." Harvey tells me, and a small laugh escapes me.

"There's that smile." Cole says softly, and my smile widens.

This is what it's like. For so many years, I've wondered what it was like to have a full family, and this is it. I don't think about dad, about the third floor or anything other than my family, and it feels nice to not be worried about when dad will hit me next or how drunk he'll be when he comes home. I let out a breath I didn't know I was holding as a weight is pulled off of my chest.

Because now, I can be a kid.

A/N: sorry for not posting this sooner, but I hope you guys like it!

Word count: 1451.

chapter twelve - custody

- -

We get back from the ice cream parlour, and Harvey, Cole and I go into the kitchen. I freeze when I see my father, Archie, and a girl I don't know sitting at the table.

My dads face is bruised and stained with blood. His lip is swollen, too.

"I'm assuming this is Annalise?" The girl asks.

"Yeah." Archie says as he motions for me to come over. I nervously make my way over to them, and my dad smiles when I look at him.

"What's going on?" I inquire quietly.

"My name is Lana, I'm from social services." She explains, and I stiffen. I look between her, Benedict and Archie. "Both your brothers and your father want custody over you, and I'm the person who decides who you stay with."

I look back at Cole and Harvey. They promised me that I would get to stay here. They promised that I wouldn't have to go with him.

Cole puts his hand on my back. "How about we go watch a movie in the film room?" He suggests, turning me around and not giving me much of a choice.

"Wait—" I begin.

"Go on, Annalise." Archie cuts me off, his voice stern. Like whatever they're talking about isn't something that I should hear. And, to be honest, I'm not sure if I even want to hear it.

"Shouldn't she be a part of this conversation?" Benedict asks. "After all, it is her life."

But, before I can be asked if I want to stay, I'm already out of the room. I don't want to even be in the same room as him, let alone sit across from him on a table talking to a girl about the possibility of having to move back with him.

––––––

Nobody's talked about Benedict since he left. I saw him leave out of he front door, and he looked furious.

There's a knock at the door, and Harvey goes to get it. I sit at the kitchen island, slurping my milkshake, and Mason and Dean walk in.

A smile immediately blooms onto my face when I see Mason, and he smiles brightly back. Then, somebody whispers something in my ear, startling me.

"Aw, the baby's blushing." Elijah mumbles, smirking. I roll my eyes, and he points his finger at me. "Attitude." He warns, and I prop my head up on my hand, annoyed.

"I wasn't giving any attitude." I whisper to myself.

"What was that?" Jameson asks from behind me, tilting his head.

"Nothing." I respond, smiling innocently.

He glares at me for a second, and then relaxes his face.

I've talked to all of my brothers and had conversations with each of them.. but not Jameson and Grayson. I don't think they like me very much. Jameson accused me of stealing his things, and Grayson was rude to me the first time he met me.

"Mason and Dean are eating with us, go say hi to them." Jameson orders, and I suddenly become nervous. He pours himself a glass of water and puts it up to his lips, but when he sees that I'm not moving, he sets it back down. "Go on."

"Do I have to?" I ask, biting my nails.

"Is little Anna scared of talking to a boy?" Elijah teases, pinching my cheeks. I slap his hands away and both of them laugh. I feel my cheeks go red in embarrassment.

"No." I mumble, hiding my blush by looking down.

"Awww, Anna, don't be embarrassed." Jameson fake pouts. "Everybody gets crushes."

"Yeah, only, if you or Mason act on those little crushes you have for each other, we'll fucking kill him." Elijah smiles, crossing his arms and resting them on the counter. My eyes widen, and his smirk grows wider.

"Noted." I respond after a few moments of silence.

He pats my shoulder. "Good."

"Dinner's ready, hurry up." Grayson says, poking his head into the kitchen and then leaving.

"You know, I'm good." I say, carefully getting down from the light grey, cushioned stool. "You guys have fun."

I'm almost out the kitchen when Jameson steps in front of me, blocking my path. I try to move past him, but he moves in my way.

"Where do you think you're going?" He asks, raising an eyebrow.

"My room." I reply, confused.

"And you're not coming to dinner why?" He inquires, crossing his arms.

"Because I'll throw up and ruin everybody's appetite?" I say.

"Not if you take two of your pills beforehand." Jameson tells me, pulling yellow bottle out of his pocket. He pours two onto his hand, and Elijah passes me a glass of water. Jameson gives the medicine to me, and I put them at the back of my tongue before swallowing them with a few sips of water.

We go into the dining room, and Cole tells me to sit in between Mason and Elijah. I slowly get over to the chair I've been assigned, and Mason turns to me once I've sat down. "Hey." He says, a small smile creeping up on his lips.

"Hi." I reply, taking my crutches off and leaning them on the wall behind me.

A sudden wave of tiredness washes over me and I yawn, covering my mouth as I do.

"You tired, Anna?" Elijah asks, nudging me. I nod slowly, blinking a few times in attempt to wake myself up a bit more. "Might be the medicine."

"Why would something that's supposed to help me, like, digest or whatever make me tired?" I inquire.

"I mean the meds for your leg from earlier." He says.

"Oh." I respond. "Maybe."

Food is set in the middle of the table, but I don't make any move to grab some like everybody else. Elijah notices and puts food on my plate for me.

"I'm not hungry." I inform him.

"I don't care, you're not leaving until you've eaten everything on your plate." He responds before shoving food into his mouth.

"But—"

"I'm serious, Anna." He cuts me off. He points at my plate with his fork. "Eat."

"Elijah—"

"Do I have to fucking spoon feed you? Eat what's on your plate, Annalise." He demands.

"You okay?" Mason asks, grabbing my attention. I turn to him, and he has the sweet smile I usually see him with on his face.

"Yeah." I say, smiling despite how sick and tired I feel. All I want to do is crawl into my bed and fall asleep.

I look down at the food, grabbing my fork, and take a few bites. I don't throw up, which I'm happy about, but I still feel like I could sleep for days.

I rub my eyes. "Can I be done now?"

Elijah sighs. "Fine. But you're having a big breakfast tomorrow."

"Okay." I mumble, reaching for my crutches.

"Come on, I'll take you." He says, standing up.

"No, it's okay." I assure him, scrambling to my feet and using my crutches to help me regain my wobbly balance. "Goodnight." I say, my voice muffled as he pulls me in for a tight hug.

"Goodnight, you little baby." He responds.

"I'm not a baby." I argue, and he laughs.

I lean the front of my body onto him as my eyes flutter closed. And I can feel myself being lifted up and carried off.

A/N: here's another chapter! Tysm for 1K READS!! I can't believe it!

Word count: 1238.

chapter thirteen - glass

I swallow one of the pills that quicken the healing of my leg while Harvey watches me like a hawk before he passes me two of my digestion pills. I look down at them and sigh before placing them at the back of my tongue and drinking some water.

I feel like a sick little girl. Though, I suppose I sort of am.

The tiredness doesn't take long to hit, and within a few minutes I'm just as sleepy as I was last night. I suddenly crave the comfort and warmth of my bed.

"You okay, Anna?" Jameson inquires, walking in.

I furrow my eyebrows in confusion.

When did he become.. nice?

"Yeah, I'm fine." I reply.

"Go back to bed, Anna. You look like you haven't slept in days." Harvey tells me.

"Because of that fucking medicine." I say to myself, lowering my voice as I jump off of the stool and get my crutches on.

"Ooo, somebody said a bad word." Cole says from beside me, and I roll my eyes.

"Hey, attitude!" Jameson exclaims. His voice is softer when he speaks next, "go back to bed, Anna."

"That's where I was going." I respond, and three sets of eyes snap towards me.

"Attitude, Annalise. Fix it." Cole demands.

"I wasn't giving any attitude." I argue, annoyed.

"Do you want us to ground you, Annalise? Because that's the path you're headed on." Cole warns loudly as I leave the room.

"Whatever!" I shout back.

Once I'm at the stairs, I realise I need somebody's help in order to get to my room. I'm stubborn, so I'm not going to ask one of my brothers for help, I'll find a way up on my own.

I look up at the spiral staircase and realise that it might be a little bit harder than I anticipated.

I try a number of different ways a few times, but I hardly make it past the third step. I look down at my cast and rip off the velcro keeping it on and take it off of my leg. I throw it on the floor, along with my crutches, and when I walk, I feel fine. It doesn't hurt. Not one bit.

I widen my eyes in surprise and a smile blooms onto my face.

I can walk.

I can walk?

How can I walk?

I'll work it out later.

I run up the stairs and sprint into my bedroom, feeling a sudden rush of adrenaline. But when I see my bed, tiredness replaces the small amount of energy I still have. I jump onto it, landing on my stomach, and darkness quickly consumes my sight.

————

The loud sound of an air horn right next to my ear wakes me up.

"Get up! You're coming to work with me!" Cole shouts over the noise. When I don't move, he drops the air horn on my bed and lifts me up, throwing me over his shoulder.

I groan and he puts me down in the doorway of my bathroom.

"Get ready and meet me downstairs in ten minutes." He orders, then looks down. His eyes furrow. "Where's your cast?"

"I don't need it anymore." I answer. He raises an eyebrow, waiting for me to elaborate. "I took it off and I could walk. It's a miracle." I smile, and he fights a smirk.

"Okay, hurry up." He tells me before walking out of my room, shutting the door behind him. I walk over to my mirror, rubbing my eyes tiredly. When I see my reflection, my eyebrows raise in surprise. My hair is all over the place, and there is crust in my eye.

I tie my hair into a low ponytail and wash my face with cold water, which helps me wake up a bit. I change into a pair of leggings and a plain, white t-shirt before going downstairs, still amazed and questioning how I can walk. The hospital must've gotten it wrong, or my leg healed really fast.

Leo's walking across the hall when I get downstairs, and he stops and looks at me.

"Where's your cast?" He inquires suspiciously.

"I don't need it anymore." I smile, and he walks closer to me.

"But your leg's broken?" He says.

"I guess it got fixed." I shrug my shoulders.

Cole says my name from where he's waiting at the front door before Leo can ask any further questions, and I walk over to him, waving goodbye to Leo.

"What will I be doing?" I inquire, a little bit nervous, as we walk out to his car.

He looks back at me for a brief moment, unlocking the doors to his expensive looking car with the press of a button on his keys. "You'll see."

I go to get in the passenger seat, but Cole shakes his head and points to the back.

"Are you serious?" I ask.

"Do as you're told, Anna." He tells me, and I roll my eyes before getting in the backseat. "And watch the attitude, how many times do we have to tell you?"

A thought pops into my head.

What if they don't keep me because I'm being rude?

Suddenly, my eyes water and I blink a few times to rid of the tears threatening to fall. I don't feel totally at home, but I've only been living with them for two weeks, maybe less. But still, I don't want to have to leave. Especially because who I might end up living with. What if they have enough of me and decide to send me back to dad?

"Seatbelt, Anna." Cole reminds me, and I quickly put my seatbelt on.

When the car starts, I'm scared. I haven't been in a car since the accident, apart from the ride home, but I was practically asleep on the drive back to the house.

We come to a halt, and I clench my eyes shut, memories from the wreck coming back to me.

I remember the blood on my face when I saw my reflection in the shattered car window. I remember Elijah's blood covered face and him holding me before everything went black. I remember how much my head hurt when I hit it. I remember the gunshots. I remember it all, and it haunts me.

"Anna." A soft voice whispers, snapping me back into reality. "Open your eyes."

I do.

Cole is turned around in his seat, and we're parked on the side of the road. I blink a few times and a tear falls, but my brother quickly wipes it away.

"You're okay, Annalise." He assures me, and I avert my gaze to the window, bringing my knees up to my chest. I hear him sigh quietly, and soon after he starts the car again.

We arrive at a restaurant, and my eyes widen.

"You work at a restaurant?" I ask, surprised. He doesn't seem like somebody who would be a waiter, or even a chef.

"I own a restaurant." He corrects me.

That makes more sense.

We pull into the car park, and he unbuttons his seatbelt, I copy him quickly and get out of the car. The two of us walk through the front door, and Cole leads me to the back.

All eyes turn to us as we enter the kitchen, and I look down at my feet, embarrassed.

"Everyone, this is my little sister, Annalise." Cole begins, wrapping an arm around me, "she'll be helping you guys out by washing the dishes. Isn't that right, Anna?"

He looks down at me, smiling, and I nod, sending a glare his way, which only makes him laugh.

He points to the sink. "Hop to it, little sis." He gives me a little push forward and leans down so that he's whispering in my ear. "Next time, maybe don't have an attitude."

I frown at him, and he winks in response.

I make my way over to the sink and sigh when I see all of the dirty dishes I'll have to wash.

————

"Hey, Anna. I need you to go take table seven's order." Cole says, walking over to me.

"Why?" I ask, rinsing a plate.

"Because I said so." He replies, handing me a notepad and pen once I've dried my hands. "Now go."

I reluctantly walk out, and when I see who's sitting at table seven, I scoff. All of my brothers, including Dean and Mason, are sitting in the large booth. As I go to go back into the kitchen, Cole grips my shoulders and turns me back round.

"Brought this on yourself, kid." He says.

He walks away, smirking, and I breathe in, preparing myself.

I slowly walk over.

"What do you want?" I ask when I reach them.

Jameson is the first to speak. "That's no way to talk to paying customers. Especially not if you want a good tip."

I fight the urge to roll my eyes.

"So sorry." I say. "What can I get you all on this fine Tuesday evening?"

"It's Saturday, Anna." Elijah says. I scrunch my eyebrows together.

Harvey and Archie share a knowing look, and I look down to the floor. I keep forgetting little things, and it's all confusing me. I just want everything to go back to normal. I want to be able to remember where my room is and if I've taken my meds today and what day of the week it is.

"Oh." I mumble quietly. "Anyway.. uh—what do you guys want to eat?"

They all order, and I write all of it down on the small, pale yellow notepad Cole gave me.

I walk back to the kitchen and give them the order before making my way back to the sink, drying the remainder of the dishes. As I go to put one back, it slips out of my hand and falls onto the floor. Without thinking, I kneel down and try to pick the shards up, and blood pours from my hands. If I don't clean it up, they might send me back.

"Fuck, Annalise!" Cole exclaims, "what are you doing!"

A/N: I honestly don't know what to write in this authors note bit anymore. But I hope that you liked this chapter :)

Word count. 1711.

chapter fourteen - home

Cole rushes me into the staff room, and messages somebody on his phone. After a few moments, the door bursts open and Archie, Harvey, Leo, Mason and Dean run in.

Dean grabs a first-aid kit that's hanging on the wall and opens it. He grabs a pair of tweezers, wipes and a bandage. I watch him carefully as he takes my hand and begins wiping all of the blood away.

Mason jumps up on the counter next to me, and he gives me a reassuring smile.

"I'm gonna take one of the pieces of glass out now, okay?" Dean says, and I nod.

"God—Anna, what were you thinking? Picking glass up off of the floor?" Cole exclaims.

"I'm sorry, I didn't want—holy crap!" I shout as Dean picks a piece of glass out of my hand. Without realising, I grab Mason's hand and squeeze it tightly. "Sorry." I mumble, embarrassed. From the corner of my eye, I see Leo and Harvey smirk.

"It's fine, don't worry." He dismisses, smiling gently.

I feel the heat rush to my cheeks and look down in attempt to hide my blush.

"Okay, second piece." Dean announces, and I clench my eyes shut.

A few seconds pass, and I open my eyes again. "I didn't feel that one."

"Because I haven't done it yet." Dean replies, amusement dancing in his eyes.

"Oh."

"Okay, I'll do it now." He tells me.

He pulls on the glass and I snatch my hand back.

"Please stop." I whisper. I get off the counter. "I'm gonna go to the toilet, I'll be back in a minute."

"Alright." Dean says, moving out of the way. I open the door and instead of going to the bathroom, I go outside.

The cold breeze hits me as soon as I step out of the door, and it's quite a relief after being stuck in the warm kitchen for the past few hours.

I walk to the side of the building and sit cross-legged on the floor, leaning my back on the brick wall. I look down at my hand and sigh. Maybe I can just leave the glass in and it'll fall out on its own.

A few minutes pass, and I hear somebody calling my name. Grayson walks around the corner, and his eyes soften for a second when he sees me. "Is this where you've been hiding?" He asks, sitting down next to me. "Everybody's looking for you."

I shrug my shoulders.

"You know, if you get it over and done with it'll be a lot easier." He explains.

I look at him, and he's lighting a cigarette. He puts it fo his lips and breathes in, then holds it out to me.

"I'm thirteen." I tell him.

He takes it back. "I mean, you can still have some—"

"I'm good." I quickly dismiss him, and he looks down.

There's silence for a few moments, and all I can hear is the rustling of leaves.

"Why'd you come out here?" Grayson inquires.

"It hurt too much." I answer.

"So your plan is to just leave the glass in?" He assumes.

"Pretty much." I reply.

"No, you're not." He says, standing up and reaching his hand out. "Get up, come on. We're going back inside so that Dean can get that glass out of your hands."

"But—"

"Come on, Annie." He demands. When I make no move to stand up, he grows impatient. "Do I have to throw you over my fucking shoulder or are you gonna get up on your own?"

Hesitantly, I take his hand and stand up.

"Good." He says.

Grayson doesn't let go of the loose grip he has on my hand as we walk into the restaurant. Cole is the first to see me, and he storms over.

"Where were you?" He asks hastily.

"I got lost." I lie, putting on an innocent smile.

"Annalise." He warns.

He looks at me for a few seconds, a stern look on his face, and I give in.

"I didn't want Dean to take the glass out because it hurts." I eventually admit, looking down. They'll definitely decide that they don't want to keep me after tonight with all of the trouble I've caused. My brothers could be enjoying their food right now if it weren't for me and my clumsiness.

He sighs. "Okay, come on." Cole says. "We have to get that glass out of your hands. And it's gonna hurt, but it'll be over soon."

Cole holds my other hand lightly and walks to the back room, taking Grayson and I with him. When we get back into the staff room, everybody's in there. They all look at me at the same time, and I feel small under all of their stares.

"Sorry for running away." I mumble, embarrassed.

"It's okay, Anna." Dean responds.

Cole lifts me up onto the marble counter again and jumps up next to me. He pulls me in for a hug, putting his hand on the back of my head, and I happily hug him back.

Then, Dean pulls a piece of glass out of my hand and I shriek, trying to get out of Cole's arms. He wasn't trying to hug me, he's restraining me.

Another piece of glass gets pulled out of my hand and I bury my head in Cole's chest, tears streaming down my face.

Cole runs his hand through my hair comfortingly. "It's alright, Anna. He's almost done with this hand, then he'll bandage it up and do your other hand."

Dean pulls the last piece of glass out of this hand and sets it in the small, plastic tub next to me. I let out a breath I didn't know I was holding as he wraps a bandage around my hand.

"Okay, hold out your other hand for me, Annalise." Dean says. Reluctantly, I bring my other hand over to him, and he wipes the blood off.

————

I can't sleep. My wrapped-up hands hurt too much, and I feel like I'm going to be sick.

I'm also scared that when I wake up tomorrow, my brothers will tell me that my time here is up.

A tear rolls down my cheek at the thought, and I feel a sudden sense of hate for myself because I'm always crying. I need to stop being so sensitive.

My door cracks open a little bit, and Leo pokes his head in. "Annalise." He whispers.

"Yeah?" I reply, sniffling.

He walks in and shuts the door behind him, turning the light on. Once he sees me, he walks over quickly.

"What's wrong, sweetheart?" He asks softly.

"Please don't make me leave." I cry out. "I'm sorry for having an attitude and I'm sorry for dropping the glass at Cole's restaurant and running away but I'll never do it again, I promise. But please don't make me leave. I like it here. Please, Leo."

"Annalise.." He whispers. "Just because you do something wrong doesn't mean we're gonna send you to live with someone else. You're not going anywhere. Ever. You're here with us now. You're home."

I smile at his words.

"Now, come on. Go to sleep. Family meeting tomorrow." He says.

I furrow my eyebrows. "Family meeting?"

"Yeah. We need to talk to you about something." He tells me.

"What is it?" I ask.

"The sooner you go to sleep, the sooner you'll find out." He says, winking at me. I frown, and he grins. "Goodnight, Anna." Leo goes to say something else after that, but changes his mind at the last second.

"Goodnight." I mumble, laying back down. I pull the blanket over me and shut my eyes as Leo turns the light off.

————

I go downstairs and walk into the living room. Everybody's already there, sitting down on one of the couches or armchairs.

"Hey, Anna. Sit down." Cole says, moving up on the couch so that there's a space between him and Grayson. I slowly walk over and sit there.

Everybody's dressed, and I'm in my pyjamas. I feel a little out of place.

"Okay, now that everybody's here." Leo begins. "Annalise."

Everybody looks at me, and I sink back into the couch, wishing that it would just open up and swallow me whole.

"Yeah?" I ask nervously, my voice so quiet I'm not even sure he heard me.

"We want you to go to therapy." He tells me.

"No thanks." I quickly respond.

"What if we give you £20?" He asks.

"Are you trying to bribe me?" I inquire.

"Is it working?" Leo counters.

"No." I reply.

"We'll give you anything you want." He tries to convince me, and I look at him with a deadpan expression.

"No." I repeat.

"You're going." Cole says from beside me.

"Am I, though?" I ask.

He glares at me, and I glare back. He raisers an eyebrow warningly, and I look away.

"Yes, you are." Grayson speaks from the other spot next to me. "It'll help you, Annie."

"Help me with what?" I ask. "I'm not crazy." I add, more quietly.

"Annie, you know what I mean—"

"No, I don't." I cut him off.

"Cole told us that you freaked out in the car." Archie says, speaking for the first time. "That and your nightmares, flashbacks, everything that happened with Benedict and the fact that you've lost some of your memory."

"That last part isn't true." I state, crossing my arms. He tilts his head to the side. "Just because I forgot what day it was once doesn't mean I've lost my memory."

"You've forgotten more than that, Annalise." Harvey says, sighing. "You're going, Anna. End of conversation."

"That's not fair!" I exclaim.

"Life's not fair." Grayson whispers, and Cole smirks.

Word count: 1630.

chapter fifteen - lectures

The one hour lecture about why I should go to therapy finally ends, and Harvey passes me my meds as I make my way out of the living room.

When I get to my room, I look at the small yellow bottle. I go into my bathroom and pour them all out onto my hand before shoving them in the toilet and flushing.

They make me feel horrible. After taking them, I always feel tired and weak. Besides, I don't really need them anymore. My leg's fine.

"Annalise." Somebody says before opening my bedroom door. I shove through bottle into my cabinet and leave my bathroom to go and see the person who almost caught me.

Archie is standing in my doorway.

"Yeah?" I ask.

"We're going to Dean and Mason's, get dressed." He orders, leaving as soon as the last word leaves his mouth and shutting the door behind him.

————

Archie knocks on the door and a short, blonde woman opens it.

"Archie! Come in, come in." She exclaims, and when she sees me her small smile grows wider. "You must be Annalise! You're so big now."

She pulls me in for a hug as everybody else walks past us and into the house. She steps back and her eyes scan over me. She takes my hand and pulls me inside of the mansion excitedly.

"Mum, let her get through the door." Dean says, coming down the stairs, and I look between both of them. It's only now I notice the resemblance.

Mason walks behind his brother and a smile lights up on his face when he sees me. I smile back, and he walks over.

"I wanna show you something." He whispers, and I furrow my eyebrows. Before I can stop it, he's pulling me down a hallway and I can help the giggle that escapes me. He turns around. "You have a nice laugh."

I'm thankful that this hallway is dark, because that means he can't see my blush.

"Thanks." I smile.

"Come on." He says, and takes my hand. We run down another hallway and stop at a white door.

"What's in there?" I ask, looking at him to find that he's already gazing at me.

"Open the door and find out." He tells me, smiling.

I grip the doorknob and turn it. When the door opens, my eyes widen. It's a cinema room, just like ours, only bigger and lit with galaxy lights. I look around the room, and two chairs with blankets and snacks catch my eye.

He walks over to them and I follow.

"You didn't have to do this.." I say quietly.

"I wanted to." He responds, and I feel myself blush yet again. He sits down and motions for me to. His seats are even comfier than ours, and it feels like I'm sinking into a marshmallow when I sit down.

"Okay, what movie?" He inquires, and pulls out three CD's.

The first is Avengers, the second is Divergent and the third is a movie I've never heard of before. I close my eyes and point to a random one. When I open them again, I see that I've chosen the last one.

"Stay here, I'll go turn it on." He tells me.

I nod. "Okay."

He leaves and comes back a few minutes later just as the movie begins rolling. I throw my blanket over me and sit back, and Mason does the same.

"How are your hands?" He asks quietly.

"They're fine mostly. Still hurt a bit, though." I answer.

He throws a piece of popcorn at me and I gasp jokingly before throwing one back. He catches it in his mouth and I glare at him, which only makes him laugh harder than he was before.

He throws another piece at me.

"You're so dead." I say, laughing.

"Oh, yeah?" He asks, and I nod confidently.

I get a handful of popcorn and throw it at him.

Before he can do it back, the door to the room opens and the sound echoes throughout the large room.

Archie and Dean stand in the doorway, and they scan the room. When they spot us, they walk over. Archie sits on the chair next to me and Dean goes over to Mason.

Archie's POV:

We got a call from security telling us that Benedict was trying to break into Anna's room with a bat and pocket knife, but he got away too soon for them to catch him.

I have all my men on lookout.

But, until he's found, I've asked Dean if we can stay with him. He said yes, thankfully, and everybody else has gone to get all of our stuff. We don't need much, because we can borrow stuff from Dean and maybe even Mason, but Annalise needs her things.

I walk over to her and Mason, thinking about what I'm going to say when I reach them. How do you tell your thirteen year old sister that her father attempted to break into her room with weapons, one of which was a knife.

I sit down next to her and take a deep breath. "Annalise."

"Am I in trouble?" She asks nervously.

I laugh softly. "No, Anna, you're not in trouble." She releases a breath. "Why? Is there something you should get into trouble for?"

Her eyes widen. "No." She responds quickly.

"Okay, good." I say. I inhale. "Annalise."

"Hm?" She replies.

"We're gonna stay here for a couple of days." I begin. "There was a.. gas leak at the house and, until it's fixed, it's dangerous to go back home."

I feel bad for lying, but I don't want to tell the truth and risk her being scared or upset when we do go home.

"What about our stuff?" Anna questions.

"Cole, Leo and Harvey went to go get everybody's things." I inform her.

Her eyebrows furrow. "But you just said it's dangerous to go back."

"They have masks." I say.

"Oh." She mumbles.

A few seconds go by, and the only sound in the room is the movie that Annalise and Mason were watching.

"There are only seven guest rooms, so you and I will share. Is that okay?" I ask.

She smiles. "Yeah, sure."

I pat her shoulder, and then silently curse myself for being so awkward.

"Enjoy your movie." I say before standing up.

Annalise's POV:

Archie and Dean leave, and we continue to watch the movie.

Mason yawns and puts his arm around my shoulder subtly. I can't help but laugh.

"Real smooth." I say, giggling. I move his arm from around me. "My brothers would kill you if they saw you with your arm around me."

He laughs a short laugh. "Yeah, they would."

He looks at me, and I swear that time stops. When his light brown eyes connect with mine I smile, and the corners of his mouth turn upwards, making my heart flutter.

————

"That was the most boring thing I've ever watched." Mason admits as we walk down the stairs, and I laugh.

"Yeah, I wish I picked Avengers now." I respond.

I hear the front door close, and the sound of Cole calling my name quickly follows. I quicken my pace and Mason leads me to the kitchen where all of my brothers are.

Cole throws me my bag that has all of my stuff in it, and I mutter a quick 'thanks'.

"Oh, Annalise." Cole says, and I snap my head towards him. "Why the fuck is the bottle that's supposed to have your pain meds in empty?"

"What?" Archie shouts.

"I can explain.." I mumble.

"Yeah, you're gonna." Leo says angrily. "Sit down." He orders, and I slowly walk over to one of the bar stools and sit on it. I look down at the ground, and when I look up again, all eyes are on me.

"Fucking explain then!" Jameson exclaims.

"They make me tired.." I whisper. "And my leg's fine now, I don't need them!"

Nobody talks for a minute or two, and the silence is deafening.

"What'd you do will the pills, Anna?" Archie inquires, pinching the bridge of his nose.

"I flushed them down the toilet." I answer quietly.

"Fucking hell, Anna." Harvey mumbles.

"I'll go to the chemist and get the bottle refilled." Archie says, grabbing his jacket from the back of one of the dining room chairs and puffing it on.

"No—you don't need to! My leg's fine. I'm fine." I try to convince him as he walks to the front door, but he ignores me. "Archie, please. I don't want them."

He turns around. "I know you don't want them, Annalise, but you need them. If I could snap my fingers and make you better, believe me, I would. But I can't, so you need to take medicine instead." He says. "Leo can take you to one of the guest rooms and we'll talk about this later. Don't think your off the hook for flushing your meds cither, Annalise. Because you're not."

And with that, he opens the door and walks out.

It's not my fault that the medicine made me tired. And it's not my fault that it made me feel weak. I hated feeling so sleepy all of the time, so I did something about it. Why are they mad about that?

"Come on, Anna. I'll take you to the room Archie normally stays in." Leo says, grabbing my bag off of the counter and flinging it over his shoulder.

A/N: I'm posting this at 3am :)

Word count: 1596.

chapter sixteen - gunshots

Leo leaves me in the guest room and I throw my bag onto the bed, sighing.

I pull out my blanket and wrap it around me before laying on top of the duvet. I slowly breathe in and out, staring at the ceiling.

Somebody knocks at the door.

"Yeah?" I say, loud enough so that whoever's on the other side can hear me.

"Can I come in?" Mason inquires loudly.

"Sure." I shout.

The door opens, and he walks in, a small—almost sympathetic—smile on his face.

"Hey.." He mumbles. He comes over and sits next to me, making the bed dip slightly.

I'm not sure if he's allowed to be here, because I can't imagine that my brothers would want me to be able to talk to somebody seeing as they're all mad at me.

"Why'd you do it, Annalise?" Mason asks, and I snap my head toward him.

He looks back at me, and I quickly look away.

"They made me tired, I hated it. I was constantly sleeping." I tell him.

"You still shouldn't have flushed them, Annalise." He says, and I can feel his eyes on me. "They make you better. What if something happened to your leg because you stopped taking them?"

"Nothing would have happened." I state.

"You don't know that." He responds.

"Yes, I do." I say. There's a few seconds of silence before I talk again. "Why do you even care? You've only known me for a few days."

"I care because you could get hurt." He tells me calmly.

"No, I couldn't!" I exclaim. "My leg is fine! Why doesn't anybody get that?"

The door opens, and we both look at Archie who has a small, paper bag from the chemist in his hand.

"Out." He orders Mason.

When Mason leaves, Archie walks over to me. I can't tell his mood, because he's hiding it so well. I wish that my most intimidating, authoritative brother weren't the best at hiding his emotions; it'd save me a lot of nervousness.

He sits at the end of the bed and looks at me.

"First of all, you're grounded." He says.

"Why?" I exclaim.

"Because you flushed your meds, Annalise. Do you realise how serious that is?" He replies. I go to protest, but he talks before I can. "You'll be supervised taking your medicine, and from now on, you'll take them twice a day."

"That's not fair!" I whine.

"It's perfectly fair, Annalise." He replies calmly.

"No, it's not!" I say. "They made me tired, so I flushed them down the toilet. I shouldn't have to take them again."

"They make your leg better, Anna. You have to take them." He tells me.

"My leg's already better!" I assure him.

"Yeah, for now!" He shouts, anger washing over him. He inhales, looking away, and then returns his attention back to me. "You're gonna take the fucking medicine, Anna."

"I don't want to!" I speak. When I talk next, my voice comes out like a whisper. "Please don't make me take it, Archie. Please."

"Anna, you have to. You can stop taking them in two weeks time, that's what the chemist said." He explains. "And these are less strong, too, so if they do make you fall asleep, it'll only be for an hour or so."

I groan and lay back on the bed.

I hear him open the bag and unscrew the lid to the bottle. He clears his throat and I look up at him. "Come on, let's go get a glass of water." He says, standing up and holding his hand out for me. Reluctantly, I take it, and he leads me downstairs.

He lifts me up onto the high counter and gets a glass out of one of the cabinets. He fills it up with water before handing it to me, along with the pain pill.

"My leg really is fine—" I begin, but Archie cuts me off.

"Annalise." He says sternly.

I roll my eyes.

"Attitude." He warns.

"Right. Sorry." I mumble quietly.

I look at the medicine in my hand and sigh before setting it on the back of my tongue and swallowing it with a few sips of water.

"Good girl." He says, lifting me back off the counter. I look out the window, and it's dark out. I didn't realise how fast the day has went. "Dinner will be ready soon. Mrs. Beckett and Cole are cooking."

"Okay." I respond, and he pats me on the shoulder before leaving.

I sigh and wait for the tiredness to kick in, but it doesn't.

"Hey, Anna." Harvey says, grabbing my attention.

I walk over and hug him. For no reason exactly, only that I'm happy. Happy to be with my brothers. Happy to have people who care about me. And happy with my life.

Harvey slowly wraps his arms around me and plants a kiss on my forehead. We stay like this for a few moments, until Cole and Mrs. Beckett come in.

"Go hug in the living room." Cole says. "We need to make dinner."

————

"Can you pass the salt?"

"Stop eating like that."

"This is nice, Mrs. Beckett."

"I helped."

A lot of people are talking. And as much as all the different, loud conversations are giving me a headache, I smile, because this is what family is like, and I'm slowly learning that.

"Whats got you grinning like a Cheshire Cat?" Grayson asks, nudging me.

I'm about to answer, but the deafening sound of gunshots cuts me off. I freeze as I watch the windows shatter and glass go everywhere.

"Annie." Somebody shakes me gently from my position under the table, and I look up at them, then at the window that isn't broken. I furrow my eyebrows in confusion. "What's wrong? What happened?" Grayson inquires, setting his hand on my shoulder.

Mason helps me up. "Are you okay?" He asks, concerned.

"I'm fine." I respond before taking a bite of my food. I look up, and everybody's staring at me. "What?"

"What the fuck was that?" Jameson inquires, breaking the silence.

Everybody looks at me, waiting for an answer, an explanation, about what just happened.

"Uh.. I'm just tired. I'm gonna go to bed." I stand up. "Thanks for the food, Mrs. Beckett. It's really nice."

"No problem, hunny." She smiles, but I can see the concern in her eyes.

"Night, everyone." I say.

I walk up the stairs, my breath quickening with each step I take, and make my way into the room Archie and I are staying in. Before

I can shut the door, Mason holds it open. I didn't even realise he was following me.

"What's wrong?" He asks, his voice kind.

"Nothing, I'm just tired." I dismiss, and I go to shut the door but he stops it from closing all the way. Again.

"Wanna see something cool?" He asks.

I cross my arms and sigh. "Can I change into my pyjamas first?"

"Yeah." He smiles, and I can't help but smile too. His is contagious.

"Okay. Wait here." I order, and quickly shut the door. I go over to my bag and pull out the first pair of pyjamas I see and change out of my white shorts and pale yellow shirt.

Mason's POV:

The door opens, and she walks out wearing a matching set of stitch pyjamas. I smirk, and she glares at me.

"My outfit's better than yours." She says, and crosses her arms over her chest.

"Yeah, your stitch t-shirt is gorgeous." I respond sarcastically, and she shoves my arm playfully. She looks away, and when she looks back, a smile is plastered on her face.

"Alright, where are we going?" Anna inquires.

"You'll have to be patient and find out." I tell her, holding out my hand. She reluctantly takes it and I lead her down the hallway and up to the roof. "Stay here a second."

I pull out two chairs and set them next to each other. I motion for her to sit on one, and she does. She brings her knees up to her chest and shivers. I quickly take my hoodie off and throw it to her.

"You'll be cold." She says, her teeth chattering.

"I'll be fine." I dismiss, and she puts the hoodie on quickly.

I pull the bottle I stole from downstairs out, and her eyes widen when she sees it.

"My brothers would kill me." She tells me nervously.

"You don't have to have any." I assure her, sitting down on the seat next to her.

I drink some, and then clench my eyes shut from the sour taste. She smiles at me, and I can tell she's debating it, but I don't say anything because I don't want her to feel like she has to. I just thought she might like it. Though, sitting here now, I'm not sure why I thought that.

"Your mum lets you drink that?" Annalise asks.

"No." I respond. "But she doesn't have to know."

"What if she or Dean comes up here?" She inquires.

"They won't come up here. Everybody's having drinks. They won't even notice we're gone. Besides, your brothers think that you're sleeping." I explain.

She eyes the bottle, then sighs.

"Can I try some? Just a little bit." She asks.

"Are you sure?" I question. I don't want her to get into trouble. "You don't have to."

She bites her lip slightly, thinking it over. She sticks her hand out for the bottle, and I pull it away.

"This was a bad idea, I'm sorry." I mumble.

She grabs the bottle from me, and at the same time, the door to the roof opens.

"Annalise!" Archie shouts as she puts the bottle up to her lips and takes the smallest sip.

A/N: cliffhanger lol.

Word count! 1643.

chapter seventeen - balance

Annalise's POV:

Archie looks furious.

He walks over and snatches the bottle from my hand. He reads the 'vodka' label, and his anger increases. If that's even possible. He looks at me, and disappointment flashes across his face.

"Dean!" He shouts, and Mason stiffens. "Found them!"

A few moments full of silence pass, and Dean comes up the stairs. He looks at us, then at Archie, then at the bottle, and his expression quickly matches my brothers.

"Both of you, get up." Dean demands, and we do. He and Archie look at each other, and it's as though they're having a secret, non-verbal conversation.

"Which one of you got this?" Archie asks.

"What do you mean? It was obviously Anna." Dean states.

"Why was it obviously Anna?" Archie asks, crossing his arms over his chest.

"Mason wouldn't do that." Dean replies.

"I did." Mason says, and we all look at him. "I brought Anna up here, I stole the bottle from downstairs and I convinced her to drink some. She didn't do anything wrong."

"Is that true?" My brother inquires.

"It's not like he made me drink it." I say. "It was my choice.."

"But the rest is true?" Archie questions hastily.

I nod, looking down.

"The two of you, go to bed. We'll have a proper conversation about this tomorrow." Dean orders.

Mason walks over to Dean, and I walk to Archie. The four of us walk down the stairs and when we're in the hallway, I speak.

"Archie." I say quietly. He looks down at me, and I take it as permission to talk again. "Can I get a glass of water before I go to bed?"

He inhales. "Okay."

He puts his hand on my back and leads me down the stairs and in the kitchen. When we get to the doorway, I see all of my brothers sitting around, some with drinks in their hands, talking while music plays.

Harvey sees me and smiles. "Hi, Anna."

"Hi." I mumble, grabbing a glass from the side and filling it with tap water. Once Archie sees that I'm done, he motions for me to follow him. We go up the steep stairs and down the narrow hallway until we get to the guest room.

I take one last sip of water before setting the glass on the wooden bedside table. Archie turns the light off, and as he's about to leave, I stop him.

"Archie."

He turns around. "Yes?"

"I'm sorry." I whisper.

He sighs and turns the light back on before walking over and sitting next to me.

Archie waits a few seconds before talking.

"How much did you drink, Annalise?" He asks.

"Only a little bit, I swear." I respond. "Not even that much, to be honest, only a small sip." I pinch my fingers together but leave a small space between my thumb and pointer finger. "Like this much."

He takes a deep breath.

"You're gonna be grounded for longer, I'm gonna take your phone, you're going to start going to bed earlier, and we'll work out something else tomorrow. Understood?" He says, and I nod. "Good."

Archie stands up and walks over to the door. He's about to turn the light off, but I stop him again. I know that I was assured I wouldn't be sent back, but I need to ask.

"Please don't make me go back." I blurt out, and he looks back at me.

"Go back where?" He asks.

"To my dad. I know I did something wrong. I'm sorry. I'll never do it again. But please don't make me go back to him." I plead.

"Anna, I don't care if you fucking kill somebody, I'm not gonna send you back. You're not leaving." He says. "Not again." He whispers that part, but I can still hear him.

———

Mason and I hand Archie and Dean our phones, and they put them in a safe.

"A safe, really?" Mason asks. "That's a bit unnecessary, don't you think?"

"It's just in case you try to steal them back." Dean tells us, shutting the door to the small metal box.

"Anna, you can have your phone back in a few days." Archie says.

I nod. I don't really care. I don't use my phone that often, and whenever I do use it, it's constantly glitching. I'm surprised it hasn't electrocuted me yet.

"Can I go back upstairs?" I ask.

"After you take your meds." Archie says, motioning to where the glass of water and pill are waiting for me on the counter.

"Okay." I fake a smile as I move past him. I quickly swallow the pill with water and grimace at the taste.

"What's wrong?" Archie asks.

"It tastes weird." I explain.

I blink, and I suddenly feel droopy. My shoulders drop, and my eyes relax.

Before I know it, I'm losing my balance. When I took the pill yesterday it didn't feel like this. So why now?

"Woah, Anna." Archie says, stopping me from falling by holding onto my bicep. "Come on, let's get you back to bed." He adds, holding my hand and taking me over to the stairs. "We'll take these bandages off of your hands soon, too."

I yawn. "Okay."

I'm just as tired as I am confused at the moment. Why did Archie go so easy on me? I'm almost positive that he knows about my broken phone, so how come he let me off so easy by taking it away? He grounded me for longer, too, but it's not like I go anywhere to begin with.

Archie opens the door for me and I mutter a quick 'thanks' before going in. I walk straight to the bed and lift up the covers, putting them back down over me once I'm comfortable.

My brother closes the curtains, blocking the midday sun from lighting up the room, and my eyes shut almost immediately. He comes over and kisses my forehead, and soon after the door opens and closes.

Archie's POV:

I walk back downstairs, and Leo comes over to me quickly.

"He's gonna get Anna." He says, and I furrow my eyebrows.

"Who is?" I ask.

"Benedict." He responds, and I stiffen.

Annalise doesn't know about her father trying to get custody, and I plan for it to be like that for as long as possible. We've promised her she's not going back, so she's not. I'll do anything and everything to ensure that. He won't take our baby sister away from us again.

Leo takes a deep breath. "His lawyer called me with an ultimatum."

I snap my head toward him.

"He wants to live with us. To be a family again." He informs me.

"Absolutely not." I state.

"Archie. He could tell the court about what we do. We'd go to jail, and Annalise would go with him or into foster care. Do you want that?" He asks, and I avoid eye contact with him. "At least if he lived with us she'd be here, and we could protect her against him. It'll be better than Anna being alone with him."

I finally look at him. "There's one more option."

"What's that?" He inquires.

"We could kill him." I suggest.

"It'd look too suspicious, they'd know we did it." He tells me.

"Not if we say that he ran out because he was afraid." I reply. "It makes sense. An alcoholic scared to get his daughter back in case he messes up again. Nobody will know that he's dead, they'll think he's ran."

"Yeah. That could work." Leo mumbles.

"We'll get him here, say we'll give this family another chance or something, and then take him to the third floor and tie him up." I explain confidently.

This has to work. I don't see a reason why it wouldn't. I'd rather die before seeing Annalise being taken away from us again.

A/N: I actually don't know what to write here anymore. But please comment and vote if you like this chapter!

Word count: 1340.

chapter eighteen - ache

Annalise's POV:

I wake up, and the room is dark and quiet. The curtains are closed and the only source of light is the little glimmer that shines through the blinds.

A sudden burst of pain rushes through my head, and I hold onto the spot it hurts most.

I stumble out of the bedroom and downstairs. When I get to the kitchen in hopes to pour myself a glass of water, Archie and Dean are having what looks to be a very serious conversation.

"Anna, what're you doing out of bed?" Archie asks me, walking over.

I blink a few times and quickly take a glass out of the cupboard. "My head hurts." I mumble, my voice so quiet that I doubt he even heard it.

He takes the glass from me and fills it up before passing it back, noticing my shaking hands. I thank him before gulping down half of the glass, the coolness calming my throat but doing nothing for my aching head.

He waits until I finished the water before speaking.

"We'll be able to go home tomorrow." Archie informs me, and a smile immediately blooms onto my face. I've missed the comfort of my own bed. Not that there's anything wrong with Mason and Dean's house, I'd just rather be in my own room.

"Really?" I ask, not being able to take the smile off of my face.

He nods. "Now, go back to bed. I don't wanna have to deal with a grumpy teenager tomorrow."

Archie ruffles my hair, and I scrunch my nose. He gives me a little shove towards the door and I make my way back upstairs.

When I get to the room I'm staying in, I see Mason sitting on the end of the bed, waiting for me. He smiles when he notices I'm here.

"What're you doing?" I ask in a hushed voice, walking over to him.

"I'm bored. Cant sleep." He explains.

"Okay.. let me be more specific. Why are you in my room at," I look at the time on my phone. "2a.m?"

"Wanna watch a movie?" He asks after a few seconds of silence.

We're already in trouble, so I don't want to get in more. Though, it is only a movie, and we'll go to sleep once it's finished.

"Fine." I say.

He jumps up from the bed and motions me to follow him. We tiptoe down a few hallways until we reach the film room.

Mason pushes open the doors and we go to a random two seats. He goes up to the front and puts a movie in while I get myself comfortable.

The movie starts rolling and he comes back over.

Mason yawns, and in the process he puts his arm over my shoulder.

"Lame move, man." Elijah says from behind us. I jump at the sound of his voice.

There's an annoyed looking, blonde haired girl sitting next to him. And she looks as though she can't wait for us to leave.

"It's 2a.m, shouldn't you both be asleep?" He asks, and Mason and I look at each other.

"Shouldn't you?" I counter, glaring at him slightly.

He raises an eyebrow. "No, because I'm not a baby. I can stay up past twelve."

My mouth gapes. "We're not babies." I say, crossing my arms.

"Yeah, okay. Go to bed." He orders, sounding bored.

"No, we're watching a movie." I respond. "Go make out or whatever someplace else."

The door opens, and Archie looks around the room, looking for something, or someone. When his eyes land on me he stops searching and pushes the door open wider.

"Bed." He demands simply. "You too, Mason."

I stand up, and Mason trails behind me while I walk over to Archie.

"But I'm not tired." I groan.

"I don't care." He states, closing the door behind us as we walk into the hall.

"How will I fall asleep if I'm not tired, though?" I question, turning around slightly as we move through the narrow hallway.

"Not my problem, princess." He dismisses, placing his hand gently on my back, leading me to the room.

————

We're home.

Archie opens the front door, and I quickly walk inside, happy to finally be back.

All that excitement is quick to disappear when I see a familiar face in the distance, sitting in the kitchen. I march to him, tears threatening to fall out of fear and confusion.

Before I can get to the man who I'm sad to say is my father, somebody pulls me back by gripping my wrist.

"Go upstairs." Archie orders. When he realises that I have no intention of following his orders, he calls Harvey over. "Take Anna to her room."

"Wait—no. What is he doing here?" My voice comes out as a mumble as Harvey lightly grips my arm, gently pulling me over to the staircase and up the steps. "Stop!"

"Bambina, don't worry about it. Let's just get you to your room and you can unpack all of your things. He'll probably be gone by dinner." He assures me.

"Probably?" I question.

We reach my white bedroom door, and he pushes it open, walking in before me and throwing the duffel bag containing my things on the bed.

"Maybe take a nap, too, you look tired, sweetheart."

The same headaches I was experiencing last night have been reappearing all day. On and off, and when I think it's gone for good, it comes back.

I hate this. I hate all of it. I despise being the sick little girl who loses her balance and gets headaches and has to take medicine just to stay sane. I feel weak. Pathetic. Small. Like I'm being pitied every time I walk past one of my brothers, though maybe I'm just being paranoid.

"Okay." I whisper, climbing onto my soft mattress and letting my head fall back onto the cool pillow.

"I'll wake you up in a few hours, okay?" Harvey asks, but I'm too tried to respond with words, so I settle for offering him a nod.

My eyes slowly begin to flutter closed, and the temptation of rest pulls me in until I'm in a deep slumber.

A/N: hey guys! I know this definitely isn't the best and I'm so sorry for not updating this in ages. I've not had the most motivation to carry this story on but I'm going to try, so I apologise if the writing becomes sloppy.

Also, my apologises for this chapter being shorter than the others.

Word count: 1093.

chapter nineteen - slaps

"Are you kidding me!"

"Anna, we'll sort it. He'll be gone soon." Archie responds, his voice stern.

"I'm not staying here while he is!" I exclaim, reaching under my bed and moving my hand around until I find the bag that contains my stuff from when we were staying at Mason and Dean's house that I have yet to unpack.

I'm glad I didn't now, though. Because that means that I don't have to pack a bunch of stuff to take wherever I go next.

"Annalise." My oldest brother says, his voice stern. A tone that I'd normally feel a sense of fear towards, but right now I don't care.

I thought that they were on my side. How can they just let him back here with the knowledge of all that he's done to me? Maybe that was their plan all along. Perhaps my father was in on it, too.

"Anna, what are you doing?" Leo asks.

"Leaving!" I respond loudly.

"The hell you are." Archie tells me.

I look back at him, my face a mixture of confusion and bewilderment.

"I'm sorry, did you expect me to want to stay?" I ask.

"I understand you're angry and perplexed, but don't forget who your speaking to, Annalise." He warns me. A few silent seconds pass until he speaks again. "You are thirteen years old, you aren't going anywhere."

I go up on my tippy-toes, making myself taller, and slap him in the face.

"You're a liar. And you're mean. And I hate you!" I yell, my voice strained and tired.

"Annalise!" Leo shouts.

"What?" I question.

He just stares at me, as though he doesn't know who I am anymore. And that's not fair, because all of them lied to me, and I'm the one who gets yelled at.

"You're lucky if I don't slap you next. You lied, too. You all did." I tell him. Another uncomfortable, short silence follows, and I talk once again. "Now can you get out? If I'm bound to this stupid house the least you can do is leave me alone for a few hours."

Archie's POV:

My heart physically hurts.

She doesn't really hate me, right?

That's just something kids say when they're angry, isn't it?

Isn't it?

"She didn't mean it, Arch." Leo assures me.

I feel pathetic. My feelings have just been hurt by my 13-year-old sister. I'm supposed to be "The resilient leader of the Italian Mafia", and I'm close to crying when my baby sister slaps me and tells me she hates me.

"I've got shit to do. Sort Benedict out. And check on Anna in half an hour." I order my younger brother, and he nods before making his way out of my office.

Annalise's words replay in my mind.

You're a liar. And you're mean. And I hate you!

I clench my eyes shut, standing up from my office chair and walking over to the door.

I refuse to allow him to hurt her again.

I quickly walk up our spiral stairs and go to Anna's room. I knock twice.

"Who is it?" Her voice questions on the other side of the white door.

"Archie." I answer. "Can I come in?"

"No." She responds.

I go in anyway. Which, judging by the glare settled on her face, isn't the best thing I can be doing to make her like me again right now. But that isn't my priority. My priority is making sure my princess is safe. Despite how much she hates me. And despite how I'd be scolding anybody else if they slapped me.

I deserved it, to be honest.

"I said no." She says.

"I know." I breathe out. I've never felt more awkward.

How is a little girl making me question myself and my emotions? My eyes haven't so much as watered since.. I don't know. But suddenly her saying how much she doesn't like me makes my eyes flood with tears?

"Get blankets, pyjamas and stuff. Anything you'll need. It's only for a few days. You're staying in my room, I'll sleep on the couch in the corner." I say.

"I'm not gonna take your bed from you—"

"Just do as you're told, Annalise. Don't worry about me." I respond quickly. "And don't push your luck."

She's already on thin ice. But I don't blame her at all for hitting me. She doesn't know anything of what's going on, and it scares her. If I were in her situation, I'd probably be confused and scared, too. She has to live under the same roof as a man who abused her. Not for long, though. And never again. Not if Leo and I's plan goes the way it's supposed to. But we need Annalise for that, but we need to figure out a way to tell her first in a way that doesn't include or bring up any questions about what I and my younger brothers do.

She sits on her bed, confusion causing a crease between her eyebrows to appear.

"Now, Anna." I specify.

She stands up and climbs off of her bed, picking up a teddy bear and two blankets. Then she moves over to her walk-in-wardrobe and comes out with a few pairs of pyjamas and a few pairs of clothes. But she normally just stays in the things she sleeps in all day, so I doubt she'll be needing anything to go out in. I'm hoping to have him out by Tuesday, anyway. And her therapy session—that she doesn't know anything about, not yet, anyway—is on Wednesday. So all should be well by then.

I open the bedroom door, letting her walk out first, and then follow her as she makes her way to my room.

When she gets inside, I motion for her to sit on the bed, and when she does, I go over to my desk, picking up the new phone I got for her, and place it on the bed next to her.

"I'll send Harvey up to help you set it up." I say before going back over to the door. "I'll be in my office. Nobody can hurt you in here, okay?"

She visibly stiffens before nodding.

Annalise's POV:

I feel really bad.

Of course I don't hate Archie. I just said that in the heat of the moment. I could never feel anything but gratitude towards my brother.

I am mad at him, though. He allowed my father back into the place I was just beginning to call home. And I do kind of hate him for that, but I don't hate him. I could never hate him. He's my big brother. I just hate and strongly disagree with the decisions that he makes.

"Hey, bambina. Got a new phone?" Harvey questions, walking into the room.

"Mhm." I mumble, pulling my two blankets over me more, keeping myself warm against the cold temperature of the room.

He sits down next to me and takes the box with a picture of a phone on the front of it, pulling the top up, revealing a large device.

For the next ten minutes, he makes me put my thumb on the home button so that the phone can recognise my fingerprint.

A/N: sorry it's taking me so long to post chapters!

Word count: 1227.

chapter twenty - phone

"Do you wanna eat dinner at the desk?" Archie asks. "I can bring it up for you."

I appreciate how he knows that I don't want to go downstairs and face my father after trying so desperately to forget about his very existence. And it makes me wonder: why would he let him come back if he knew that this would be my reaction?

He doesn't try to convince me to see him. And he's doing a lot of things to ensure that I don't have a chance to. So it causes me to question if he even had a choice in his return, or if it simply happened and there was nothing he could do. Although, it is Archie. Just him raising one of his eyebrows at me in warning is enough to scare me.

"Yes please." I mumble, scrolling through my new phone, looking at all of the apps.

Harvey was downloading stuff for me, and when I asked him about social medias and if he could download some of those, too, he said no. Because apparently 'apps like Instagram and Snapchat rot your brain.'

I don't really understand what he meant by that, because being on your phone claims to do the exact same thing, yet I still just got a new one.

I protested and said that I used to be allowed to have it, but he told me that if I'm in their house, then I have to abide by their rules. And I told him that was stupid, and he said he didn't care.

Then he finished setting up my phone before leaving.

My oldest brother opens the door, shutting it after he steps out, but not before sending me a small glance that has an ounce of hope clinging onto it. Hope that I'd say something, I think.

I planned to, but he left too swiftly for me to apologise for what happened earlier.

A few minutes pass, and he comes back, this time with a white plate in his hand and a glass of water in the other.

He sets them down on his wooden desk, leaving again after.

It makes me wonder if he's mad about what happened. Probably. I did slap him. And I also told him how much I hate him. And called him names. But what did he expect me to do? I know that it may not have been the best approach, but I was scared. I didn't know why he let my father here, so slapping him was what my brain told me to do. But now my brain is telling me that I should go apologise.

Which, after I finish the food I can manage to stuff my mouth with, is the reason I venture out into the hallway.

I slowly walk through the second floor, making my way down the spiral stairs and scanning the space I end up in with my eyes, ensuring that my dad is nowhere in sight. When I determine that he isn't, I hastily make my way to my brothers office.

I knock, over and over again, looking around, paranoid incase my dad just suddenly appears.

Archie opens the door, and I look at him.

My eyes widen.

It's not Archie.

It's my father.

Suddenly, memories come back to me. Ones of him hurting me, ridiculing me and pushing me down the stairs.

"Annalise." He smiles.

He doesn't smell like alcohol, which is strange. And he isn't wearing dirty clothes. These are new. Made of a rich, kind-on-the-eyes material.

"Anna, go upstairs." My brother says from behind him.

"Am I not allowed to speak to my own daughter?" He responds.

"No, because she's gonna go watch a movie with Elijah." Archie replies.

Elijah walks out from behind both of them—all of them must have been having a conversation—and stands next to me, immediately leading me away by gently gripping my wrist and pulling me to the movie room.

"Come on, princess." He says softly, urging me forwards.

I keep looking behind me, a chill running down my spine at the smirk my good-for-nothing father sends me before shutting my eldest brothers office door.

Elijah stops and tilts my head up so that I'm looking at him.

"Don't worry about it, Anna." He tells me quietly. "He'll be here for a few days, max. You have nothing to be afraid about."

I stiffen. Of course he thinks that. He doesn't know what I've had to endure while living with him. He doesn't know about how many nights I've slept with a homemade shiv under my pillow. He doesn't know how many times I've cried myself to sleep in fear and sadness and confusion.

He doesn't know about how many times I've wished that I could just have a dad who loves me.

I slap him, too.

I'm on a roll today. First Archie and now him.

"Fuck you, Elijah." I say.

I know he'll tell Archie. And if he doesn't punish me for slapping him and telling him that I hate him, then he definitely will for slapping somebody again and swearing.

I don't really care right now, though. I don't have time to. Because I'm already halfway up the staircase when I slowly start to realise just what I've done.

I don't think he meant it to be rude. He was just trying to assure me that I have nothing to worry about. Which isn't true, either.

I have everything to worry about now that he's back in my life.

———

"Annalise!" Archie shouts, walking in. "Are you kidding me? Why do you keep on slapping us?"

"Because you all deserve it." I respond honestly.

A few days ago, I would've taken that comment right back and begged him not to send me away. But I hope he does, now. It'll be better than staying here with my dad.

He raises an eyebrow warningly, not liking my answer, and I flick my gaze away from him, focusing on my phone, instead.

He snatches it out of my hand, and I look at him, confused.

"You're grounded. Again. And I'll be taking this." He tells me.

I've only had it for a day!

"Sort your attitude out, Annalise. And maybe you'll get your phone back." He tells me. When he speaks next, his tone is pleading. "What's going on with you?"

A lot, I suppose.

"Nothing." I mumble, crossing my arms over my chest and leaning back so that my head is resting on the pillow.

"Annalise!" He shouts. "I asked you a question."

"And I answered you. You just didn't like my response." I say.

He inhales a sharp breath, rubbing a hand over his jaw. When he turns to me again, his eyes are full of frustration.

"Here's what you're gonna do." He begins. "You're going to go and apologise to Elijah, and then you're going to stop slapping everybody, alright?"

"No."

"No?" He questions.

"Nope. I'm not going to apologise when I'm not sorry." I reply.

"Oh my—Anna. I'm not asking." He tells me sternly.

"I'll do it if you give me my phone back." I say.

"Are you trying to negotiate with me?" He inquires.

"You're very perceptive." I compliment.

"Annalise. Go downstairs. And go apologise. You're not getting it back until you do." He warns.

And with that, he leaves.

A/N: two chapters in two days? Who is she???

Word count: 1245.

chapter twenty one - blade

A fter he leaves, I cry. But I don't know why tears are streaming down my face or why I'm suddenly so upset.

Everything about today has just been so confusing. I'm scared and puzzled and worried and—

My door opens.

"You haven't came to say hello yet." My father says.

Fear slowly begins to build up inside me as he shuts the door. But the thing that really makes me want to scream in terror is him turning the lock, giving me no way out.

He inches closer, and my breathing becomes heavy.

"What're you doing?" I ask, my voice trembling with terror.

He makes his way over to me and when he's standing next to me by my bed, he strikes his hand across my face, leaving a harsh sting.

"What did I tell you would happen if you ever told anybody about what I did to you?" He questions.

I feel my whole body shaking out of fright. Out of worry.

"You'd kill me.." I respond quietly.

"And I'll make good on my promise." He assures me.

He pulls something out of his pocket and then presses a cold, metal blade up to my stomach. He turns it over tauntingly, and I clench my eyes shut.

"Look at me. I want to be able to see you when I kill you. To watch the life drain out of your eyes." He whispers, and his low voice sends shivers down my spine.

"Dad, please." I choke out, a stray tear rolling down my face.

The doorknob twists, and then there's a knock on the white door.

"Annalise! Why's the door locked?" Elijah shouts from the other side.

I pluck up all my courage and grab my fathers hand, turning it and sending the knife into his arm. He cries out in pain and I run to the door. But before I can unlock it, I'm pulled down to the floor by my hair.

"Help!" I scream.

Benedict covers my mouth with his hand, muffling all of my attempts to shout for help.

A sharp sting presents itself in the lower part of my stomach, and I cry.

He jumps up and runs over to the window, unlocking it quickly and jumping out.

I look down, and crimson blood is seeping through my shirt, dying my white top a horrible colour of red. I cover the wound up with my hand and manage to stand up. I slowly walk over to the door and unlock it, then fall straight to the ground again.

"Anna!" Elijah exclaims, kneeling next to me. He turns around, "Archie! Leo! Somebody!"

My eyes fall shut while my big brother cradles me in his arms.

————

I'm completely alone.

I'm in a hospital bed, and nobody's here.

"Archie?" I whisper, frantically searching the room with my eyes. "Elijah?"

Where is everybody?

A lonely tear rolls down my cheek as I look down at myself. There are tubes sticking out of my body, and monitors beside the bed I'm laying on. Just like when I was here because of the crash. But it was different then, because people were here for me. But now nobody is.

I rip the plastic out of my arms, crying quicker now. I need to find my brothers—if they're even here. And if they even care.

I get up off the uncomfortable bed and walk over to the door, opening it slowly.

I ignore the pain in my abdomen as I walk through the narrow halls, desperate to find a familiar face. But eventually, I give up, and sit on a seat in one of the waiting rooms, bringing my knees up to my chest and crying into them, the sound of my sobs being muffled.

"Annalise?" I snap my head up towards the sound of the familiar voice.

Harvey.

I cry even harder, and he makes his way over to me, sitting on the blue chair by my side and holding my hand in his, tracing small circles on the back of it.

"What's wrong, bambina?" He asks softly.

"I woke up and everybody was gone." I tell him. "I didn't know where I was, and nobody was there to tell me."

His eyebrows furrow in concern and sadness and worry. But then he pulls me in for a warm hug, rubbing his hand over the small of my back. He plants a kiss on my forehead and looks down at me.

"The nurse told us you wouldn't be awake for a few more hours, so we all split up, decided to do our own thing and get food until you woke up." He explains. "If we knew that you'd be awake none of us would have ever left your side." Harvey assures me, and I begin to feel a little bit better. "Now come on, let's get you back to bed. You shouldn't be walking, you might open your stitches."

"Stitches?" I whisper to myself as he lifts me up off the chair, cradling me like a baby.

I let out a small giggle, and he looks down at me, confused.

"You have a moustache." I inform him.

He only looks up, a small, amused smirk on his face, and shakes his head.

He walks in silence for a few minutes until we reach the familiar hallway and stop outside of the hospital room.

"Thank fuck, you found her!" Archie exclaims. He opens the door and Harvey carries me inside, gently placing me down on the bed.

Archie sits on one of the couches across from me and begins to talk.

"I understand that you might have been afraid when you woke up, but you're not in a state to be walking around." He explains. "Okay?"

I nod.

"Use your words, Anna." He tells me.

"Yeah, okay."

"We're gonna leave in half an hour or so, alright? But we're not going home. We're going on a little trip. Mason and Dean are coming along, too." Archie tells me.

"What about Mrs. Beckett?" I ask.

"She's gonna stay home." He says. "Everybody else is at the house packing up our stuff, so when they get here, we're gonna go."

"Don't you need to wait until the hospital discharges me?" I question.

"The hospital can't know about this, princess. It's just gonna be our secret, okay?" He explains, his voice patronising, but begging me to understand.

"What's going on?" I inquire, beginning to worry. "You're scaring me.."

Harvey puts his hand over mine, warming my cold fingertips up. "Nothing, bambina. We're just going on a little trip. Everything's fine."

"Then why do you need me to keep it a secret?" I inquire. "Are we leaving because of me?"

"No, sweetheart. And we're not leaving. We'll be back. But for now, you just need to trust us. Can you do that?" Archie says.

I look down at the duvet underneath me. "Yeah."

Harvey smiles from beside me. "It's all fine, Anna. You don't need to worry about any of it."

I try to match his smile, but it's an uneasy one.

I trust them, of course I do. But I don't know why we have to suddenly go on a trip or why they won't tell me much about it. Or why Mason and Dean are coming. I don't have a problem with them—and I enjoy Masons company—but I'm still unsure why they are going to be joining us.

Though, Dean is one of Archies good friends, so perhaps they're coming because they're close family friends.

"Yeah. We'll bring some pain meds, too, just in case you need them." Archie adds.

"Where are we going to go?" I ask.

Both of my brothers share a look, and I furrow my eyebrows.

"Uh, it's a surprise." Harvey eventually answers.

A/N: things escalated quickly. Where do you think they're going and why?

Word count: 1313.

chapter twenty two - blood stain

"Okay, let's go." Archie says, reading a message off of his phone and standing up from his seat.

I got changed into comfortable clothes—a white tracksuit—that Harvey brought for me a few minutes ago. He said that he doesn't know how long we'll be on the road for, so I need to be snug.

I get down from the tall bed with the help of Harvey, pressing my hand over the spot where my father stabbed me in attempt to ease the pain.

"You okay?" Harvey asks.

"Yeah." I respond.

"Annalise. When we get to the car you need to go into the very back seat by Jameson, alright?" Archie orders.

I frown. "But Jameson hates me."

Harvey looks over at me. "Why do you think that."

"Dunno, he just does." I reply.

"Jameson doesn't hate you, Anna. He just has a hard time showing kindness." Archie tells me.

I shrug. "I guess."

We reach the doors to the staircase, and Harvey holds them open for me. After muttering a quick 'thanks', we quickly walk downstairs and make our way out to the car park.

"That car over there." Harvey whispers, pointing over to a long, black, limo-looking vehicle.

The three of us walk over to it, and when I open the door, there are so many seats that it resembles a minivan.

I climb through the seats until I reach the very back—just like Archie said—and take my spot next to Jameson, avoiding all eye contact with me as I fasten my seatbelt.

I turn my phone on and scroll through all of my apps, trying to decide which one to use to occupy myself for however long we're going to be driving.

———

"How are you feeling?" Harvey asks as I get out of the car. This is our third stop, and we've been driving for an hour or two, and still, nobody will tell me where they're going.

I know that I was told not to worry, but I can't help it. My older brothers told me that it's not because of me, but they never mentioned a trip before today. Before I got stabbed by my own father.

I look up at him. "Fine."

"Anna." He says, voice holding a hint of warning. He looks away, and his eyes soften when he returns his gaze back to me. "I can tell that something's on your mind. Talk to me."

"I'm fine." I tell him as we begin to walk towards the gas station. He shoots me a doubtful look, and I sigh, deciding to change the subject. "Why won't anyone tell me where we're going?"

He visibly tenses, and I furrow my eyebrows.

He coughs. Once. "We told you, bambina. It's a surprise."

"Okay.. why are we going?" I ask.

"It's a surprise."

I roll my eyes. "Where are we staying?"

"A hotel, I think."

I look up at him. "So you don't know either?" I ask.

"You're reading too much into that, Anna." When he sees my annoyed expression, he's smirks, exhaling, before carrying on. "We've told you, you don't need to worry about a thing. We're just going on a little trip."

"Yeah, but it just doesn't make any sense!" I exclaim.

"What doesn't?" He asks, opening the gas station door and holding it for me.

"You take me out of the hospital when I haven't even been discharged, tell me we're going on some trip and don't tell me where, and then won't answer any of my questions about it!" I say. "Why can't you just tell me?"

He turns around to me abruptly in a magazine aisle, and I look at him, waiting for him to speak.

"I've told you, bambina. Archie's told you. We all have. It's a surprise. It's just something to try and make you feel better. We invited Dean and Mason along because we all know you have a crush on Mason—" I cut him off.

"I do not." I defend.

He tilts his head and grins. "Come on, Anna."

I cross my arms over my chest. "I don't have a crush on him."

He arches an eyebrow, calling out my lie. No, it's not a lie. I don't have a crush on Mason. He's my friend, yes, but I hardly know him. Sure, he's handsome and funny and sweet and—

Oh my god.

I like Mason.

"You just realised you do, didn't you?" He questions. I glare, and he laughs. "Wipe that glare off your face, bambina." In a playful tone, he adds: "your boyfriend's coming."

"What?"

I turn around and, sure enough, Mason is walking towards me, a smile on his face. A beautiful, absolutely jaw dropping smile. One that's contagious, and makes my lips turn up in the corners.

"Hey, Anna." He says.

I feel warmth spread to my cheeks, and silently curse myself for being so obvious. He said two words. Two words is all it takes to turn me as red as a tomato.

He stares at me for a moment, confused, and that's when I realise that I haven't responded. I'm just looking at him, admiring him and I probably look like a weirdo.

"Hi." I respond nervously.

He tilts his head to the side, something close to concern filling his expression.

"Are you okay?" He asks.

"Yeah.. why wouldn't I be?" I respond.

"You look pale." He glances down, and his eyes widen. "Shit, Anna!"

I follow his gaze down to my previously white jumper, now crimson red with blood. I look up at him, unsure of what I'm supposed to do, as my stomach begins aching horribly that I clutch onto the area, which only makes it hurt even more.

Harvey turns back into our aisle and he has the same reaction as Mason. He drops his chocolate bar and rushes over to me, standing behind me so that I'm able to lean on his front.

He looks over at Mason.

"Go and get someone, quick!"

He runs out of the shop and before I can figure out what's going on, my eyelids become so heavy that it's a struggle to keep them open for any longer.

A/N: sorry for not updating for so long, I haven't had much motivation or known what to do/what to write.

Word count: 1056.

chapter twenty three - screams

A nnalise's POV:

"She's waking up."

"Go get Archie."

"Why do I have to?"

"Just go, Harvey."

I hear someone sigh, then the sound of a door being opened and shut gently. My eyelids flutter open and closed, adjusting to the bright light shining in from above me, as a horrible ache starts in my head.

"Hi, sweetheart." Leo says, sitting on the bed next to me. His eyes soften when mine scrunch in agony, and he presses the back of his hand to my forehead, checking my temperature. "How are you feeling?"

"My head hurts." I groan. His eyes fill with sympathy as he moves his hand to mine, holding onto it and giving it a reassuring squeeze.

I try to sit up, but he gently pushes me back down by my shoulders, lightly shaking his head.

"Maybe you should go back to sleep for a few more hours. You look really pale." He suggests.

I shake my head. "No, I need—"

I attempt to sit up once again, but he reacts the same way he did before. He pulls a blanket over me and lays down next to me, pressing a kiss to my forehead.

"Sweetheart." He begins, voice soft. "What you need is sleep. You're tired and—"

"I'm not tired!" I exclaim, pulling my hand out of his and successfully climbing out of the bed I'm in.

"Annalise." He warns, voice sterner than I've ever heard it to be.

I don't listen to him, though. I only keep on stumbling towards the door and open it with shaky hands. Even as I hear his loud footsteps advancing towards me.

I don't want to stay in bed. I don't want to be treated like a broken doll. I don't want bad things to happen around and to me. I just want to have a normal life where normal things happen. Not where I'm stabbed by my own father or where I get into a car crash and lose a portion of my memory or where I find out that I have a bunch of brothers I never knew about.

I just want to be a normal kid. I want to do normal things that don't include going to God knows where!

Is that seriously too much to ask for?

When I finally manage to get the door open, I use up all of my energy by running across the hall and splatting against the wall. I hardly manage to hold myself up, but, by some miracle, I do. But then two arms wrap around my waist and hoist me up into the air.

I yelp in surprise, my legs dangling and two feet away from the floor. I look up at Leo, who's pivoting and walking straight ahead, towards the room I just left.

"Get off!" I exclaim. I squirm around in his grip, but he doesn't let go. Not even a little bit. "Leo!"

"Calm down, Anna." He whispers, voice soft.

"No, put me down!" I shout.

"Sweetheart, stop." He says, his tone more stern than before.

A few sets of loud footsteps walk towards us, and I use all of my power to try and unwrap Leo's arms from around me, but they won't budge. He only holds onto me tighter each time I try to get him to put me down.

"Annalise." It's Archie, I realise. And he's storming towards us, plucking me out of our brothers grip and holding me in his own. He rubs his hand up and down my back, trying to soothe me, but it doesn't work. I feel like I'm a baby throwing a tantrum. "Princess, you should be in bed." He tells me, his tone steady and calm.

"Put me down!" I exclaim.

"Anna, what's the matter?" Archie asks.

"Nothing, just let go!" I shout.

Thankfully, he does, placing me on the carpeted floor carefully as though I'm a piece of china that might break if he uses too much force.

He kneels down so that his height is closer to mine, and he's about to say something before I beat him to it.

"Don't patronise me." I say simply before walking away, back to the room I woke up in. I lock the door behind me and flop back onto the bed, which was a horrible mistake, because it makes my stomach hurt.

"Annalise!" Archie shouts, jingling the doorknob.

"Go away. I'm going to sleep!" I exclaim, my words muffled by the pillow my face is practically inside of.

"Sweetheart, you need to unlock the door. It's dangerous." Leo shouts.

I fall asleep to the sound of people yelling at me to let them in.

————

"Anna."

Someone rubs their hand up and down the length of my back, and I stir.

"Bambina." Harvey whispers in my ear.

Slowly, I open my eyes. My brother is looking down at me, disappointment obvious in his expression. It comes back to me slowly—me running away, locking the door, my brothers trying to get me to come out.

Wait. If I locked the door, how is he here?

He sighs. "You can't lock the door like that, Anna. What if there was a fire? How would we have gotten to you?" He asks.

I sit up. "How did you get in?"

"The hotel gave us a spare key." He tells me. "But that's not the point. You can't just do that and expect us to be fine with it. What happened? Why were you so upset?"

I lay back down, and he pulls the blanket up so that it covers my whole body.

"I just want everything to be normal." I mumble.

"What do you mean?" He asks.

"I want to have a dad who doesn't try to kill me, brothers who aren't clearly hiding something from me, and just a normal life where I don't lose my memory and where we don't go on random trips." I sit up again to look out the window above the bed I'm on. "Where are we, anyway?"

"Some hotel we found. We've not reached where we need to be yet. And, Anna, I understand that this might all be overwhelming for you. A matter of weeks ago, you were in a whole other environment with different people. It's a change. A really big one, and I understand it may be difficult to adjust, but this is our life, and you're going to have to get used to it."

A/N: sorry this chapter is so short! Thank you so much for 40K READS!'

chapter twenty four - pool

Annalise's POV:

"Stay in bed, sweetheart. I'll bring whatever you need to you." Leo says.

He's been coddling me all day, not leaving me alone for more than a few minutes at a time, and whenever he does, he sends someone to stay with me as though I need a babysitter.

"I'm fine, Leo." I say. I go to pull the covers off of me, but he sets his hand on top of them firmly, sending me a stern, I'm-not-joking look.

"No, Anna, you're not. You're going to stay here for as long as we tell you to, okay? No running out of bed or leaving your room in the middle of the night, do you understand?"

Something about his tone sets me on edge. Makes me feel uneasy. Normally, whenever Leo talks to me, his voice is soft and, most of the time, patronising. So it's weird, and a little bit scary, that he's talking to me like this, over something as simple as staying in bed.

Despite wanting to ask him about all that, I just nod. I want to go to sleep anyway, but I want to be alone. I doubt he'd ever let that happen, though, because he has been protective—more than usual—of me today, and didn't even let Jameson in when he wanted to see me.

I thought that was strange, too, because Jameson hates me. He doesn't talk to me, he doesn't smile at me, and the only nice thing he's ever done is ask me if I was okay when we were in the car, but that was probably just because I had just gotten out of hospital, and I suppose he felt bad.

He's refused to let Mason in, too. Who's one of the only people I actually want to see. He's the only person my age, and the only person who's any fun. But my brothers won't let me—despite how much I've asked. They said that Mason and I tend to get into trouble whenever we're together, and how that's the last thing I need.

I asked them how they know what I need if they're not me, and they told me that they're my guardians, so it's their decision. I said "but it's not your life, it's mine. I should get to be in charge of it." And they said. "Yeah, and you are a little bit, but you're under our care so you do as we say." Then they made me take some stupid medicine, along with the one for my leg which I see no reason for.

"Good." Leo says. "Do you want to watch TV, or do you want me to get you something from the bags we packed for you? A book, or something?"

"Yeah, can you get me a book?" I ask.

He smiles softly. "Sure, sweetheart. I'll be back in a few minutes, okay. I'm going to leave you alone, but so help me if you even think about running away I'll make sure you're bored out of your mind for the next few days, okay?"

I don't say that I'm already bored out of my mind, because then he'd do that stupid brother thing where he raises an eyebrow in warning and I become nervous. So instead, I nod. And only when I hear the sound of nothing, indicating he's far enough away so that he won't hear me, I stand up, untangling myself from the sheets, and slowly walk out.

It doesn't take me long to find Mason, and, thankfully, he's alone.

"Mason." I say, and he looks up at me, a grin breaking out onto his face.

"Your guard let you out?" He questions, I laugh.

"No. He left. Do you know if this hotel has a pool?" I ask.

"I think so. But, Anna, I don't know if you—"

"Great. Let's go."

"We don't even have swimsuits, and what if you—"

I cut him off a second time. "It's fine, we'll just swim in our clothes and get changed later. Come on, I don't know where it is, so you have to show me."

He looks wary, but I send him an encouraging smile and he finally stands up. He sends me a concerned look.

"Are you sure you wanna do this? You should really be in bed."

"You sound like my brothers." I tell him.

He sighs. "I just don't want you to get hurt. And, Anna, maybe we should wait a little bit. You're—I mean, you started to bleed out of nowhere a day ago, and—"

"If you don't want to go swimming with me, you don't have to. I just thought it would be fun, is all." I say, looking down at the floor.

"Fine, I'll come. But we're only staying for a few minutes. If anyone finds out—"

"I'll take the blame, don't worry."

"I was going to say that we'd both be in big trouble, and that we probably wouldn't be allowed to talk to each other for a few days."

"If that happens, then we can FaceTime." I say, and he grins. I have to fight the urge to swoon.

"Okay, come on." He says, leading the way.

The hotel we're in is massive and fancy. The room that we have is like the entire floor of an apartment. Mason and Dean share a room, Elijah and Jameson share a room, I have my own (lucky, I know, but it's probably just because I'm the only girl), Harvey and Cole are sharing and Leo and Grayson and Archie all have their own.

It's really cool. Archie told me that we're staying here for a week or two, but still won't tell me why we took this spontaneous trip. Reasons have been itching at me all day, ones like: they're in the Italian mob, and they're trying to catch an enemy (this seems very unlikely, though, because my brothers are incredibly kind. And kind people aren't in the mob, I don't think) or they actually do just want me to be able to have fun, even if they won't actually let me do anything.

Or maybe they just want us to get away without anything happening. I believe that we're safe here, that no one can get to me, and even if they did, I have hope that my brothers will protect me.

When we get to the door, the one next to it opens, revealing Jameson. He walks out of the bathroom, ruffling his wet hair with a towel with one hand and using the other to keep the one around his waist secure when he almost jumps out of his skin, surprised to see us.

He peers his eyes at me. "Shouldn't you be in bed?"

"Shouldn't you be wearing a shirt?"

He looks down the hall, then at Mason, then at me. Then at Mason again before he finally settles his gaze onto me.

"Where are you two planning to go?"

"Up your—"

"Annalise!" Leo shouts from down the hall. He storms towards us and I look at Mason, wide eyed.

"Run."

He pulls the door open and, because we're on the very top floor where the pool is also located, runs down the hallway after grabbing my hand, helping me to quicken my pace.

We burst through the doors, but stop suddenly when I see Archie. With a girl. In the hot tub. Because its on the opposite side of the large room, he doesn't hear us come in. So I press my finger to my lips, signalling to Mason to be quiet, as we round the space until we're next to Archie and the woman.

"Who's your girlfriend?" I ask, and he jumps, as does the lady. She has long platinum blonde hair that's dark at the roots and is so long it almost reaches her bum.

"You're supposed to be in bed, Annalise."

"Who is she? Holy shit, is she your kid or something?"

"No. She's my baby sister."

"I'm not a baby." I say.

"Hm." He hums. "Why aren't you in bed?"

"I am in bed."

"What?" He questions.

"What?" I repeat.

"Annalise, you—"

"—are the best sister in the world? I know. Is she your girlfriend? How long have you known her? What's her name, even? Why are you in the hot tub when it's so hot outside? Are you not burning? Can you buy me a swimsuit? I want to go swimming. Also, can you tell Leo to leave me alone? He keeps trapping me in my room—"

As if on cue, Leo opens the double doors again, and Mason and I duck.

"They're over here, Leo!" Archie shouts, and my brothers footsteps echo throughout the space.

"Wow. Wow. You traitor. Am I not allowed to spend time with my big brother? Or is your girlfriend more important than me?"

He gives me a don't-be-stupid look. "You should be in bed, Anna. You're lucky I'm not dragging you there myself, and you'll also be lucky if Leo doesn't lock you in your room and throw away the key."

"Can't I stay here?" I ask, giving him puppy dog eyes.

"No, princess." He goes to pull me in for a hug, but I move away quickly.

"You're going to soak me in your hot tub juices!" I exclaim. "These are nice pyjamas."

"There's a stain on them." He says, mildly disgusted.

"I spilt water." I roll my eyes.

"Attitude." He warns.

I notice Leo getting closer and closer.

I turn to his girlfriend. "What's your name?"

"Melody." She says, smiling.

"I'm Annalise. This is Mason." I turn my voice into a whisper. "You know, Archie already has a favourite person, and that's me. So don't think I won't fight you to make sure it stays like tha—"

Archie looks amused. "Anna. I'll be back in soon, okay? We can watch some TV and get room service. Whatever you want."

"Can we get ice cream?" I ask.

"I meant actual food."

"You just said, and I quote, 'whatever you want.' That includes ice cream."

"If you eat all your food then you can have ice cream, okay?" He says.

I glare. "Whatever."

"Annalise." Leo says. "Come on, let's go. You too, Mason. What did I tell you?" He asks me.

"You told me a lot." I reply as he motions for us to follow him. "I didn't listen to most of it, I'm sorry."

He sighs. "I know you're bored, but when I tell you to do something it's the right thing to do, okay? I'm just looking out for you, sweetheart. And, as for you," he turns around to Mason, "stop trying to take Anna on little adventures when she needs to be in bed."

"He didn't. It was my idea to go to the pool. He said we shouldn't, actually. Don't blame him."

"Oh. Sorry, Mase. I guess don't follow Anna when she's bored. Just run away from her, actually. She'll probably get you into trouble."

"Hey—" I begin.

Leo wraps an arm around me, pulling me towards him. He stops and crouches so he's closer to my height. It really gets on my nerves when they do this because it makes me feel like I'm three feet tall. Just because I'm short, it doesn't mean I'm a Smurf.

"Don't run away like that again, do you understand? You scared me." He says.

I actually feel bad now. I just wanted to have some fun, not scare him. "I'm sorry.."

He presses a kiss to my forehead. "It's okay."

This is why they couldn't be in the Italian Mob—they're too kind.

A/N: HEY! I'm so sorry I haven't edited this story for ages. I feel bad because I know a lot of people have asked for updates but I've had a lot going on.

This is longer, so I hope that it'll be good enough until the next chapter which I'm going to start right now!

chapter twenty five - sorry

Annalise's POV:

While Archie and I have been getting along, we have yet to talk about the fact I hit him across the face and then told him I hated him.

I don't; I'm certain he knows that. But I still haven't apologised. I know it's late, because I told him all this a matter of days ago, but I still want to say sorry. I don't know if my words bothered him or not, but he seemed upset afterwards, and for that I feel horrible.

An hour passes until Archie comes into my room. His brown hair is damp, but he's in actual clothes now, not just a pair of swimming trunks.

Leo—who's trying to plait my hair because I couldn't manage to without a mirror, but he won't let me go to the bathroom if I don't need a wee—looks up at him.

"What're you doing?" Archie asks.

"Sh, I'm going to lose my focus." He says.

A few seconds pass until he grins and ties the end of the plait he just made with a thin bobble. He puts it on my shoulder.

"Thanks." I smile.

"No problem. I'm a natural." He winks.

"It took you thirteen tries—"

"That doesn't matter."

I press my lips together and look at Archie.

"Can we watch TV and get ice cream now?"

"No, but we can watch TV and get dinner." He says.

I cross my arms. "No thank you."

"Anna. Come on. You can have ice cream after your dinner." He tells me.

"No. I want it now."

"You can't have it now, Annalise. It's dessert, and if you don't hurry up and come out with me, you won't be getting any ice cream at all."

I sigh, standing up and walking to his side. He nods, silently telling me that I made the right choice and leads me out into the living room area, where there are two velvet couches: one an L shape and the other small, only able to fit three people facing the large television.

I sit down on the larger couch, taking a blanket that's folded in the corner and spreading it across my body, suddenly cold. Archie sits down next to me, wrapping an arm around my shoulders and rubbing his hand up and down my upper arm. He holds up a menu that must have everything you can order on it, and then folds it open.

"What do you want?"

"Ice cream."

He sends me an annoyed look, and I smile sweetly, trying to convince him without words to let me get ice cream.

"No."

"Please."

"I said no, Anna. Pick something proper to eat."

I sigh, pointing to the chicken nuggets. He nods, picks up the phone and then orders his food and mine. When he sits back down next to me again, I hug his arm and hide my face is his shoulder.

"Hey, what's wrong?" He asks softly.

"I'm sorry for saying I hated you. And for slapping you." I blurt out. "I don't. Hate you, I mean."

He looks relieved, as though he's been waiting for me to say those words for ages.

"It's okay, princess." He presses a kiss to my forehead, turning the television on. "What do you want to watch, hm?"

I shrug. "I don't mind."

"What else is the matter?" He asks.

"Nothing."

"Anna." He says. "Come on, talk to me."

I exhale, shrugging. "I just.. I don't know. Can I go to sleep after we eat?"

"Of course, sweetheart. Do you feel okay?"

"My head hurts."

It has been ever since I woke up, but I've held off on telling anybody because then they'd treat me like "the sick girl", which I've grown so accustomed to being within the past few weeks. First it was the car crash, then the whole flushing my pills thing, now getting stabbed.

My brothers are overly baring, and when I even have so much as a temperature they treat me as though I'm suffering from a deadly disease.

I itch my arm roughly, because the ting just won't go away and it's getting on my last nerves. Archie, seeing this, slowly lifts up my sleeve before his eyes widen. He pulls my hand away, and I furrow my eyebrows.

"I think you have chicken pox."

"What?" I look down at the new bundle of red spots gathering on my arms. "Oh my God!"

"It's okay, you'll be okay. Dean!"

Dean emerges from his room, a pale looking Mason behind him. He ruffles his brothers hair.

"I think Mason has—"

"Chicken pox?"

"Yeah, how'd you know?"

He pulls up my sleeve, showing all the red spots to Dean. He looks closer, grimacing.

"I've had it before, so I'm safe."

"Grayson and Jameson haven't, I don't think."

I close my eyes for a second as the urge to itch my arms grows more and more intense. I scratch them gently, hoping that fulfils the itch, but it doesn't.

"Anna, don't, that's only gonna make it worse." Archie says, holding my spotted hands in his. "Can you see any oven mitts and tape anywhere?"

———

I can't use my hands. Mason and Dean put oven mitts on us, then secured them around our wrists with tape.

I'm now sharing a room with Mason—after a lot of protests from Archie and Cole—because we need to be "quarantined" to make sure that we don't spread it to anyone. It'll be nice, being able to talk to Mason, especially after my realisation that I have a crush on him, but I've been cooped up in my room for days, and I don't want to have to be any longer.

Damn you, chicken pox.

I'm trying to rub my back up and down the end of the bed, and Mason is attempting to use the carpet to fulfil his itch, but I don't think it's working for him. It's not for me, either, not unless I press really hard, but that hurts.

The door swings open, and Archie and Cole walk in. They look at us on the floor, helpless, and Cole laughs.

"You guys look sad."

"I will give you chicken pox." I say.

"I've already had it." He replies.

"Some people get it more than once. Maybe you will too."

He looks at Archie. "Do they?"

Archie shrugs. "Probably."

Cole walks out of the room, and I hear him shouting something along the lines of: "someone get me a fucking hazmat suit."

Archie kneels beside me. "Anna, sweetheart, remember what I said? Itching is only going to make it worse. Leo's getting some cream to make it a bit better, but you just have to try not to for a few days, okay?" He explains. He lifts me up by my underarms and then sets me on the queen sized bed. There are two in the room; one belongs to me, the other belongs to Mason. My stuff is on the floor next to mine, all folded and ready to be put into drawers.

I folded and unfolded and then refolded all of my clothes. I thought that if I did something to occupy myself then I wouldn't want to crawl out of my skin, but that didn't work. So now I have a bunch of folded clothes and nowhere to put them, because there isn't even a dresser in here. There's only a small wardrobe that's already occupying Mason and Deans stuff.

"It hurts." I whine, kicking my legs like a toddler throwing a tantrum.

"I know, princess, I know. But it'll be okay soon. You'll get through it, Anna. Try get some sleep, okay? You too, Mason—why are you sliding on the floor?"

"To itch."

Archie pulls Mason up and directs him into his bed. He walks back over to me and presses a kiss to my forehead before turning the light off, leaving us alone.

A/N: two chapters in the space of a few hours? Who is she??

chapter twenty six ♥ care

Archie's POV:

After leaving Annalise and Mason to sleep, I go back into the living room and put the food my sister and I ordered into the microwave; she can eat it when she wakes up.

I walk over to Leo and Grayson, who are sitting on the couch. I know what they're talking about before I even have a chance to listen.

"Any updates?" I ask, standing behind them.

"We've had to pay a lot of people off, but a woman said they saw him go to a motel a few days ago. It's called 'The Cage.'" Harvey explains.

"What?"

"Yeah, I know. Weird name. Anyway, we looked inside, asked for his room and stuff, said we were his friends who were joining him on the trip. When we got to his room, it was empty and we saw a bin on wheels driving away. I got the license plate, though. S12L MHA. We're tracking it now."

Grayson shows me an iPad with a Google maps type set out on the screen. There's a blue dot driving through the streets quickly.

"And you're sure that's him?"

"Well, ninety percent sure. We've never saw his face, but the room and the lady—"

"Let's go, then."

"Where?" Grayson asks.

"To find Benedict?" I say like it's obvious, but they seem confused.

"Arch—" Harvey begins.

The front door to our hotel room is pushed open. It falls off its hinges as our father walks in, a gun in hand and several men behind him.

"What the fuck?"

"Where's Annalise?" Benedict asks.

"Why? Do you wanna finish the job?" Harvey asks, now standing next to me. So is Grayson.

"Go get your fucking sister."

Questions race through my mind. Why is he here? Why isn't he in that car Grayson and Harvey were just tracking?

"That's not gonna happen." Grayson says, pulling his own gun from under his hoodie. Where or when he got that, I don't know, but I'm just grateful that we have some form of protection.

"You're outnumbered." He checks behind him, and I do a quick count of the people he has on his side. Six people who are siding with a man who attempted to kill his own daughter. "I'll tell you again—go and get Annalise. She's coming back with me."

"The fuck she is." Grayson dumbly shoots him in the leg, basically declaring war.

While Benedict let's out a sound of struggle, clinging onto the spot he was shot tightly as blood pools out onto his hand, the loud bang alerts more people.

"What the fuck—" Leo says, pausing in the doorway to his room. Soon enough, everyone is in the living room, and I just cling onto the hope that Annalise and Mason are still asleep.

We have one gun between us, and they all have one of their own. But I notice how the shortest of them's hand shakes as he points the gun to my chest. I move out of the way, and decide to go easy on him since he's clearly never shot anything in his life, maybe apart from the trunk of a tree.

I walk over to him, bend his wrist until he's screaming, and then take his gun, shooting his leg before pushing him out of the still open door. He falls on his ass, and I give him another flesh wound for good measure before helping Harvey with our father.

I kick him in his leg as Harvey punches him across the face. He falls to the ground, and is quick to recover but we keep him down. I shoot him, right in the chest, before I hear a small sniffle.

My head snaps towards Annalise, who's wide eyed and is looking at me like she doesn't even know who I am while our fathers life is draining out of his eyes from under me.

"Anna—"

And then I'm shot, too, in the stomach.

Annalise's POV:

"Archie!" I shout, running to my big brother. I feel sick, and like I could die any minute, but I need to go to Archie.

Before I can get there, two arms lock around my waist and pull me back, hoisting me up in the air and into Cole's clutch. He tightens his grip as I wriggle around, sending me a warning look that I ignore. He leans closer to me as more people are shot and as Dean and Leo tend to Archie, who's on the floor trying to bite back his screams.

"Calm down, Annalise. It's going to be okay, Archies going to be fine. But right now, I need you to listen to me, okay?"

"I—"

"Anna."

I stop squirming. "Okay."

"Good girl." He says quietly, carrying me back to my room, blocking the view of what's happening with his large body and his head. He sets me down on the edge of the bed. "You need to go back to sleep, okay? Archie will be just fine, but you're sick, munchkin, you need to get some sleep."

Ignoring how he called me "munchkin" (ew), I cross my arms over my chests and nod. I shuffle to the end of the bed, oven mitts still secured on my hands so I can't itch. He pulls the covers over me, and I can't help it: I let another tear slip.

Cole wipes it away quickly. "It's gonna be fine, kid. Just go to bed, okay?"

"But, Archie—" I choke out.

"Will be okay. I just told you. Shut your eyes and go to sleep." He orders, more strictly this time.

So I do. I hope that I'll wake up and this will all have just been some horrible nightmare as I slowly let the temptation of sleep lure me in.

chapter twenty seven - movie

- -

A rchie's POV:

Everything is black. I can hear Anna sobbing, and it breaks the heart I didn't even know I had before she came back to us.

I try to open my eyes, but it's as though they're glued together. I try to move my fingers, to sit up or talk to tell her that I'm okay. I want to wipe the tears off her cheeks, but I can't. I can't help her.

Annalise! I try to scream, but no words come out. It's okay!

"Anna, you shouldn't be in here." It's Cole.

"Why isn't he awake yet?" She shouts. "You said he would be fine! Why isn't he awake yet?" She repeats the question over and over again, and I want to tell her that I am. I want to tell her to stop screaming because she'll lose her voice. I want to tell her that I am fine—that I will be fine.

"Jameson, take her to her room." Cole orders.

"No!" She squeals.

I grunt quietly as Anna argues and cries. I'm able to twitch my fingers within a few seconds, and then my eyes open. It takes me a hot minute to recognise the burning pain in my abdomen, and when I do I clench my jaw to keep back the screams desperate to escape my mouth.

"Archie!" Annalise exclaims. She kicks her way out of Jamesons grip and comes running over to me, wrapping her arms tightly around my neck. I muster up a smile when she pulls back.

"Hi, princess."

She grins. "I knew you'd wake up!" Then, quieter, "I knew you wouldn't leave me."

My expression softens. I'm about to tell her I'd never leave her when Leo steps in front of her. "Go get Dean." Leo tells her, voice strained and tired and stressed, because of me.

"But—" She stops protesting when I give her a stern nod; she looks annoyed as she stomps out of the room.

"Benedict?" I question as soon as she's gone.

"Dead." He answers. "Anna saw. All of it, then we had to drag her into her room and lock her in while we cleaned everything up. Mason stayed with her, though. She calmed down after a while."

My heart breaks when I think of Anna, begging to be let out of her room. But then anger replaces it—they locked her in a room with a boy?

"Are you feeling okay?" He asks.

"I feel fine." Pushing myself up and leaning against the headboard, I push the duvet off of me and climb out of bed.

"Archie—"

"Don't you dare try fuss over me." I let out a small, dry laugh, pushing myself to my feet. It takes me a second to regain my balance, but when I do I feel fine.

"We started the kids on a homeschool program thing. To distract Anna, mostly, but—"

"Hey, look who woke up." Dean says, sauntering into the room. He furrows his eyebrows. "You definitely shouldn't be standing."

I shrug. "I'm fine. I need a piss, though."

"Arch—"

"And food. Is there anything in the fridge? Room service takes too long."

I walk over to the door and walk out, ignoring the horrible pain in my abdomen.

"Archie—" Leo is following after me, but I'm already locking the door to the bathroom and turning the sink on to splash my face. But when I look at the mirror above it, my expression dims. I'm pale—so pale that you would think I haven't seen the sun in weeks. Months. Years.

Shuddering, I piss and then walk back out, making my way over to the fridge and pulling it open. There's nothing there, so I go over to the phone and order a pizza.

"Go back to bed, Archie." Dean says. "You can watch a movie with Annalise or something. She's missed you a lot. And you need to take things slow. You shouldn't even be standing right now—"

"I'm fine. I told you that." I tell him. "I'm waiting for a pizza."

"For fucks sake, Archie, go back to bed. Your little sister is scared shitless, and you running around everywhere isn't going to help that. So go back to bed and let her watch a god damn movie with you."

I pause. Then nod. Anna—I should be with my little sister. How did I not realise that? I should've been looking for her ever since she was sent out of the room.

I walk to Annalise's and Masons door, knocking once before pushing it open. My baby sister is sitting on her bed, and Mason is sitting next to her. Far too close for my liking.

She looks over her shoulder and at me, a smile brightening her face. She stands up, runs towards me, and wraps her arms around my waist. It takes everything in me to suppress the pained grunt rising up my throat, but I do, and then hug her back.

"Do you wanna watch a movie for a little bit?" I ask her, running my hands through her brown hair. She nods, and I can feel her smile. "Okay." I grin. "Bye, Mase." I say as I walk out, pulling my little sister to my side. We go into my room, and I pull the covers up so she can get under, then slide under the sheets myself, wrapping my arms around her. She lays her head on my chest, and I rub my hand up and down her back. "Pick whatever you want, princess." I say, handing her the remote. "No chick-flicks, though. I can't stand them."

She grins, and puts Netflix on, scrolling through the movies and TV shows before finally picking on one.

I tuck her to my side and press a kiss to my forehead, trying to distract myself from the unbearable pain in my stomach by focusing on the movie.

chapter twenty eight - beanbag chair

- -

Annalise

"Come on, bambina." Harvey says, walking into the room. I look up at him tiredly, head still resting on my oldest brothers chest. "Time for bed."

I furrow my eyebrows. "Why can't I stay here?"

"You have to sleep in your own bed, kid, come on." He says. He walks around the bed and pulls the covers off of me.

I look at Archie and frown. He just smiles, kisses my cheek and says, voice soft: "I'll see you tomorrow, baby."

"But—"

"Go, sweetheart. We can watch something else tomorrow, okay?"

Still frowning, I nod, climb out the bed, and let Harvey wrap an arm around my shoulders. I lean on him, only now realising how tired I am. While I haven't had to take my medication anymore so I'm not that sleepy during the daytime, I've been tired a lot recently.

Maybe it's because of the worry over my brother—or perhaps I just haven't been getting good sleep knowing that Mason is merely a few feet away from me.

We've grown closer in the past week. He's let me cry on his shoulder more than once, and has cheered me up more times than I can count. We've sat on my bed doing our homeschooling, and we helped each other when the other didn't know what the hell was on the worksheets we were filling out. When I wasn't allowed out of the room because of something happening with Archie, Mason pried as much information as he could out of one of my brothers or his own.

Opening the door to the room Mason and I share, Harvey steps aside so I can walk in. Mason isn't here, and Harvey checks the hallway before shutting the door again and crouching so his height is closer to mine, and a stern expression suddenly takes over his soft one.

"I'm going to trust that you and Mason keep far away from each other at night?"

I fight the urge to laugh.

"You guys are the ones that made us share a room."

"So something has—"

I don't bother to hold in my giggle this time. "No! God, Harvey, that's gross, I'm thirteen."

He breathes a sigh of relief. "But you have a crush on him?"

My eyes widen as a brush creeps onto my cheeks. "What? No!"

"Good. You're not allowed to date until you're thirty." He says. I scowl, and he laughs. "Get changed and go to bed." He orders, standing to his full height.

"No one else is going to sleep yet."

"Maybe, but you are." He smiles.

"I am not. Can we go to the pool?"

"No."

"Can you ask Cole to make me some food, then?" I ask.

"Why don't you want me to make you food?" He questions, brows furrowed.

"You always burn everything." I reply.

"I do not." He says.

"Yeah, you do." I tell him. I smile sweetly. "Please? I'm hungry."

He sighs. "Okay. But after you eat—"

"Yeah. Straight to bed, I promise." Another innocent smile.

He's about to say something when the door opens and Mason walks in. He smiles, but it fades when Harvey sends him the stern expression he was giving me before. He looks at me for a second, and I shrug. His smile brightens in something similar to amusement.

Before leaving, Harvey gives me a warning look and a kiss on my head and merely nods to Mason, who furrows his eyebrows when my brother leaves, the amusement still shining in his eyes.

"What was that?" He asks, laughing softly.

I shrug. "I have no idea."

Even though I do.

He nods, then sits on my after I do. I turn to him, smiling. "We never got to go in the pool."

He grins. "You want to now?" He assumes.

"Yeah. I asked Harvey, but he said no. So we just need to sneak out of the hotel room for a little bit."

"How do you plan to do that?" He questions.

Five minutes later, I'm running out into the living room, screaming. "There's a spider! Help!"

"What?" Jameson and Elijah—the only people in the way of the front door—look over at me.

"There's a huge spider! Please go get it!"

Rolling their eyes, they walk past me and into the bedroom. Mason grins at me and we both run to the front door, unlocking it quickly. We sprint down the hallway, but stop when I see Harvey, leaning against the wall with Cole standing next to him. They look at us expectantly.

"Next time you guys wanna make a plan to sneak out," Cole says, putting the cigarette he's holding up to his mouth and inhaling the smoke, then blowing it out, "don't talk so loud. The walls are thin."

I frown.

"Go to the pool for half an hour. But as soon as you get back to the room, you're both going straight to bed." Harvey says. I grin.

They follow us as we run to the pool, and while we discard the clothes hiding our swimming suits onto the tiled floor, Cole and Harvey sit on chairs on the edge of the pool.

Then we dive in. And when we emerge from underwater, we're chuckling. And all I can focus on are his dimples, his smile, his laugh.

He stops for a second, staring at me, and I quickly say: "wanna race?"

"Get ready to lose." He says, smirking.

•

I squeeze a towel around my hair, getting all the water out. I got out of the shower a few minutes ago, and Mason is in it now.

I walk out of the room and into the living room, the overwhelming scent of weed hitting me. I look at Jameson, who has a joint in his hand, and roll my eyes, pinching my nose so I don't have to smell it.

He looks over at me, an emotion I can't place in his eyes, and motions for me to come over to him. Hesitatingly, I do.

I sit on the edge of the couch, and he just looks at me for a few seconds before saying: "I'm sorry I've been such a shit brother."

"What?"

He blows more smoke out of his mouth and leans back. "I used to be your favourite, you know. When I was learning to read, I'd read stories to you. You'd sit next to me on the little beanbag chair in your room and cling onto my arm. Every night," he says sadly. "I'd read to you every night until our mum told me we had to go to bed. Elijah would tease me for it, but I didn't care. It was our time to spend together."

I stay silent.

"Anyway. I'm sorry I blamed you for taking my weed. I'm sorry I haven't made you feel welcome. Overall, sorry for being a dick."

His eyes soften. "You didn't deserve to be treated the way I treated you. I'm just—you used to be my favourite person. I'd get home and you'd do your little baby-waddle towards me." He laughs softly. "I guess I just didn't want to get close to you again and then you were taken away from me." His voice breaks on the last few words, and he blinks, clenching his eyes shut for a second before reopening them. He smiles at me—a genuine, happy smile that softens his usually sharp expression. "I've missed you. A lot."

And then he pulls me towards him and wraps me in a hug. I ignore the strong, overwhelming scent of weed and slowly wrap my arms around his waist. His stiff body relaxes, as though he was scared I'd shout at him, and he tightens his grip on me. Then presses a kiss in my hair.

I smile.

CPSIA information can be obtained
at www.ICGtesting.com
Printed in the USA
LVHW051130070223
738796LV00015B/1689